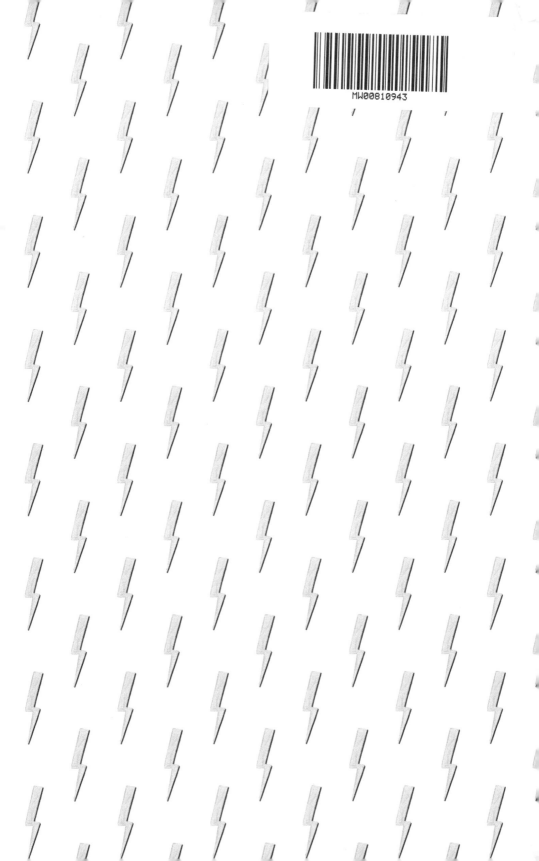

MW00810943

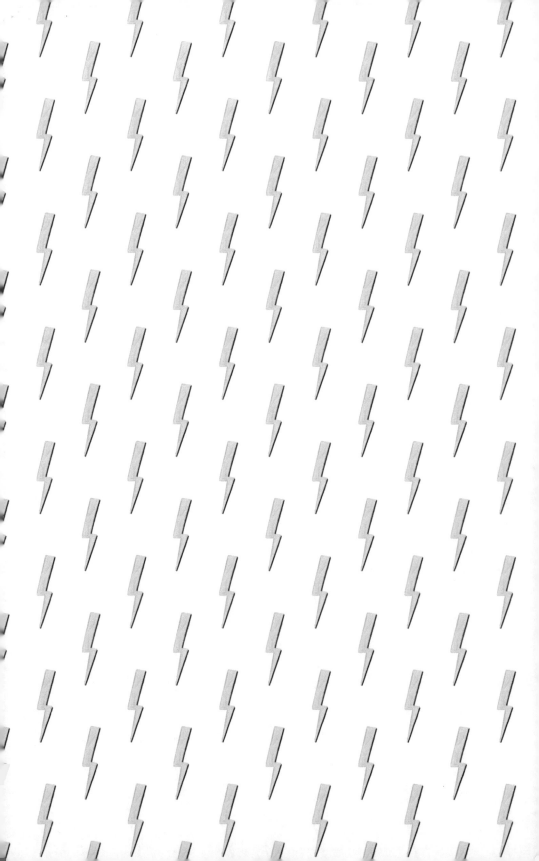

CHART SPARK

Harness your creativity in data
communication to stand out and innovate

ALLI TORBAN

DATA LITERACY
PRESS

First edition published 2023
by Data Literacy Press
500 108th Ave NE, Suite 1100, Bellevue, WA 98004
https://dataliteracy.com
https://chartsparkbook.com

Library of Congress Control Number: 2023922316

Description: First edition. | Bellevue: Data Literacy Press, 2023

ISBN: 978-1-960907-05-9
ISBN: 978-1-960907-06-6

Cover design and interior graphics designed by Alli Torban

Printed in the United States of America.

For my dad, Troy,

who taught me to take pride

in everything I do.

Do it well and do it right,

even when nobody's watching.

This book is a companion to an online course at
https://dataliteracy.com/chart-spark

Contents

WELCOME!

I'm so glad you're here.

I'm Alli Torban—an information designer and data literacy advocate based in Washington, DC. I'm also the host of the popular podcast *Data Viz Today*.

This probably isn't the first creativity book you've picked up. I don't know about you, but I'm tired of hearing creativity be conflated with artistry and reading inspirational Steve Jobs quotes. So, what makes this book different?

This book is specifically written for data professionals looking to communicate more creatively. This is your metaphorical lightning rod, ready to help you generate fresh ideas. It has actionable prompts to start using today, not just glossy pictures to admire. Now's the time to take an active role in your creativity.

Let's go!

PREFACE
Is this book for you?

If you answer yes to any of the following questions, then you're in the right place:

- Do you want to visually communicate data in new, impactful, and creative ways?
- Do you want to be valued for the way you think, not how well you use software tools?
- When you see someone else's creative work, are you overwhelmed by how such an idea even began?

Years ago, I'd have said yes to all of these. As a data analyst searching for a more fulfilling career where I could express myself creatively, I often found creative ideas would surface randomly or exclusively for other people—the "creative types."

But the issue wasn't about identity; it was about passivity. I was passively waiting for a lucky strike of inspiration to be creative. Over time, I've learned that the most creative data communicators work at it. They jump in and experiment. So, if you're ready to get to work and take an active role in your creativity, then this book is for you.

I'll help you…

- See creativity in a new way
- Care for your innate creativity
- Use prompts to coax it out when you need it
- Generate new ways to communicate your creative ideas

By the end of this book, you will feel empowered to create.

Where does this advice come from?

I led my own professional transformation from a data analyst running SQL queries all day to a creative information designer. I've also spent hundreds of hours interviewing and collaborating with creative data communicators. Much of this took place on my podcast, *Data Viz Today*, and within the *Elevate Dataviz Learning Community*, a membership for data visualization practitioners that I cofounded.

This book is a concise blend of these unique experiences, lessons, and insights. Picture it as a buffet of ideas and prompts for you to play with and make your own.

Now, I want to warn you again: This is not an "inspiration book" with pages of glossy infographics. I include some to illustrate a particular point, but the goal of this book is to change the way you think about creativity and show you how to integrate it into your work.

My promise to you: If you're ready to make your own professional transition, then I know you'll gain the confidence to create new and exciting work. Best of all, you'll also discover that you've always been the "creative type."

A reading plan

I recommend reading the whole book by following this one-week reading plan below, and then pick it up in the future whenever you feel overwhelmed or need to reference a prompt. The estimated total read time is about 2.5 hours.

DAY 1: *Estimated read time: ~25 minutes*

- Introduction: What is creativity and why should you care?
- Section I: CARE—Introduction

DAY 2: *Estimated read time: ~30 minutes*

- Chapter 1: Expand your mental boundaries
- Chapter 2: Cultivate your inspiration

DAY 3: *Estimated read time: ~20 minutes*

- Chapter 3: Build your habits
- Section II: COAX—Introduction
- Chapter 4: Blast through project paralysis

DAY 4: *Estimated read time: ~20 minutes*

- Chapter 5: Immediately see through a new lens
- Chapter 6: Find stories like an editor

DAY 5: *Estimated read time: ~20 minutes*

- Section III: COMMUNICATE—Introduction
- Chapter 7: Find an appropriate balance

DAY 6: *Estimated read time: ~25 minutes*

- Chapter 8: Explain it with a visual metaphor
- Chapter 9: Mix different mediums and experiences

DAY 7: *Estimated read time: ~10 minutes*

- Conclusion: What should you do next?

Download a free PDF of all the prompts:
https://chartsparkbook.com/journal

INTRODUCTION

What is creativity and why should you care?

What's creativity?

Creativity is the ability to generate new ideas or remix existing ideas that are useful, although its usefulness might not be immediately apparent. This ability can be strengthened through practice.[1]

1. Adapted from Fisher, R., & Williams, M. (2004). *Unlocking Creativity: Teaching Across the Curriculum.* Routledge.

CREATIVITY

Generate variations or remix

Original to me or others?

Meaningful and ethical?

Figure I.1: Illustration defining creativity. Adapted from Fisher and Williams' *Unlocking Creativity: A Teacher's Guide to Creativity Across the Curriculum*.

An idea is still creative even if it's only new to you. We often think that an idea must change the world for it to be "creative," but that's not the case. Let me prove it to you.

You don't need to be a creative genius

One day after school, my daughter pulled out a self-portrait that she painted in art class. I gushed, "Wow, that's so creative!" Her eyes sparkled with excitement, and she asked, "What's your favorite part?"

Taking a moment to consider, I replied, "I really love the way you used different colors for the shadows. It makes the piece look unique." To my surprise, she asked, "You haven't seen that before?"

I paused. I *had* seen it before, but not from her. She'd discovered this technique herself through her own exploration. If I told her that I had seen it before, would she make the mistake of discounting her artwork as *not* creative? I know that I've done that to myself a thousand times. I've taken away my "creative credit" once I discovered that it'd been done before.

Why do we hold our creativity to such high standards?

Figure I.2: Person looking to jump the impossibly high bar of creativity.

Research by James C. Kaufman and Ronald A. Beghetto[2] reveals a new model of creative acts. They were frustrated that we typically view creativity as either small daily acts or genius acts like Einstein. Through their research, they defined four types of creative acts: mini-c, little-c, Pro-c, and Big-C.

2. Kaufman, J. C., & Beghetto, R. A. (2009). "Beyond Big and Little: The Four C Model of Creativity." *Review of General Psychology*, 13(1), 1–12. https://doi.org/10.1037/a0013688.

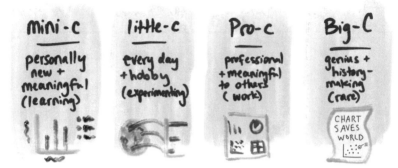

Figure I.3: Illustration of the four types of creative acts, adapted from research by Kaufman and Beghetto.

- **mini-c:** Doing something new and meaningful to you personally. Typically expressed while you're learning something new. This is the type of creativity that my daughter displayed in her multicolored shadow artwork. Maybe you finally figure out how to create a chart in Excel that solves the exact problem you're having.

- **little-c:** A creative act that builds on what you've learned and may be of value to others. Perhaps my daughter combines the shadow technique with another technique that her whole class begins to use. Maybe you figure out that you can export a map and connect it to a bar chart and it's exactly what you need. Someone else could use that idea, but they don't have to.

- **Pro-c:** A creative act that's valuable to others on a professional level. Now my daughter is an artist who consistently creates and sells art that her customers love. Maybe you add a chart to the company dashboard that no one's tried before and saves the company time and money.

- **Big-C:** A creative act that has a long-lasting contribution to society. Now my daughter's art is a permanent exhibit in museums and referenced in art textbooks. Maybe your chart is on the front-page news, and it changes the world!

With this new model in mind, how could we possibly hold ourselves to the impossible Big-C standard of creativity right out of the gate, or at all, really? It's unfair at best and harmful to the advancement of our field.

We need creativity to innovate, but if our standards are so high, then who would even try? The key is to acknowledge where you are in your creative journey and do more creative acts so that they can build on themselves.

Perhaps you tinker with one skill because it's fun and that's all. Maybe you tinker so much that one day you find yourself making little-c creative acts. Or you could be in Pro-C right now, focusing on experimenting with mini-c and little-c creative acts that will push you into Big-C. But there's no rule that you must stack creative acts with the goal of advancing from mini-c to Big-C. The point is that there's value in all creative acts whether you're looking to move through this model or not.

Stop holding yourself to the "creative genius" standard and start moving your creative acts forward in a way that's meaningful to you. Learn new skills and tools, experiment, mix and match, collaborate, share, and do it all over again. It's all creativity.

 Every creative act has value and can help you build a fulfilling creative practice in data communication.

Figure I.4: Illustration of a person jumping over the creative high bar.

Why you need creativity

 "Creative individuals play a critical role in society by driving technological innovation, advancing scientific theories, and evolving culture."
— Kaile Smith et al. in "The Creative Life"[3]

There's a give-and-take with creativity. Innovation is crucial to our society, but that's just one of the positive outcomes of creative acts. There are also negative outcomes to trying something new, like too much creativity can lead to inefficiency. Going with "what works" can be an efficient route, but it can also lead to stagnation.

Figure I.5: Illustration of positive and negative outcomes of doing creative acts versus doing things the standard way.

3. Kaile Smith, Alan Pickering & Joydeep Bhattacharya (2022). "The Creative Life: A Daily Diary Study of Creativity, Affect, and Well-Being in Creative Individuals," *Creativity Research Journal*, 34:4, 460–479, DOI: 10.1080/10400419.2022.2122371.

We struggle to balance these outcomes all the time in our work. Is now the time to try a new solution? We'll explore this more in chapter 7, but the bottom line is that even though there are negative outcomes to creative acts, there are also many positives. To help us navigate the unpredictability of creative acts, we must develop our own creative practice.

What's a creative practice?

 A creative practice is a set of skills and attitudes that helps you generate new and useful ideas in a sustainable way.

Put another way, in *The Writer's Practice,* John Warner says, "A practice consists of the practitioner's attitudes, skills, habits of mind, and knowledge."[4] Having a creative practice helps you keep going in the face of struggle. Here are important beliefs and attitudes in a creative practice:

- Creativity isn't an identity; it's an act that requires active work.

- All creative acts have value and build on each other.

- Creativity can be different from artistry. It's about how we think and act.

- Creativity has its own rhythm, and it needs care.

4. Warner, John (2019). *The Writer's Practice.* Penguin Random House.

- Habits keep us focused and confident as we navigate ambiguity.
- Prompts help us get started generating new ideas.

Don't worry if you don't know how to act on all these beliefs yet. The next chapters will give you the knowledge and tools you need. For now, the first step is to realize that data communicators have a creative practice that keeps them sane and productive. It also takes time to develop your own creative practice. You'll have to experiment with some habits and routines to find what works for you. It took me years to develop my creative practice. (If you don't care for personal stories, feel free to skip to page 27.)

How I found my creative practice

When I hit 30, my career was fractured. I had stepped away from the workforce for a year when I had my second daughter, and I second-guessed that decision every day.

Here's something I learned really fast: There's no "work-life balance." It's more of a "work-life tug-of-war." One day I felt like I was pulling for Team Career, and the next I was pulling for Team Mom.

Figure I.6: Illustration of a career woman and mother playing tug-of-war.

In reality, I didn't have a clue what I was doing on either team. Before kids, I was already struggling to figure out my career path. As a business systems analyst, I was testing software and running SQL queries from dawn till dusk for government clients in Washington, DC.

There was one particular morning I remember vividly. I was sitting at a government employee's windowless desk to troubleshoot an error with the software.

Actually, I wasn't sitting. I was kneeling on the ground in my skirt and heels while she sat in her chair sighing loudly while I tried to figure out the problem. She was running behind on her task, leaving little room for patience as I attempted to troubleshoot. Not a minute later, she let out an audible huff, snatched the bag of donut holes from her desk and barked, "Just figure it out!"

I sat back on my heels, staring at her trash can. Stressed and deflated, it hit me: I was in the wrong place. When I got this job, I felt like I was in the exact *right* place. I was supporting the government, doing important technical work. But at that moment, I knew I needed a change.

What skill was I missing to get a job where I was more valued and fulfilled? Knowing how to use a software tool wasn't doing it. I wanted to be valued for my ideas. Maybe I needed more education? I'd always been drawn to maps, with their functionality and beauty, so I decided to study at night and earned a graduate certificate in geospatial intelligence. Along with my math degree, that ought to boost my value to find a fulfilling position, right?

I applied for and landed a new job in the geospatial information systems (GIS) field, but I never got to see if my hunch was right. The same week, I found out that I was pregnant, and I felt Team Mom tugging for the first time. I decided to stay at my old, creatively unfulfilling job and go part-time so I could have a flexible schedule while I figured out this mom thing.

After keeping my head down for two years, my second daughter was born and I stopped working completely, having to figure it out again (spoiler alert: "figure it out" isn't a destination). I convinced myself that the extra space from work would help me find where that fulfilling job was hiding. I tried a few experiments, like being a part-time research assistant at a start-up and I wrote a couple of data journalism articles for a local magazine that included some data analysis and mapping.

Doing the math, I made about $2/hour on those data stories and realized two things: Freelance data journalism didn't look promising as a career path for me, but I also really liked this thing called data visualization! It included math, mapping, data, and something that I later identified as creativity. I could communicate information in ways people hadn't seen before. I could feel the potential of being valued for how I think and form ideas. It felt perfect for me.

I valued data visualization, but would the data visualization field value me?

To learn more about the field, I turned to podcasts, which was the perfect medium when my hands were tied most of the day with diaper changes and feedings. It was my beloved connection to the outside world. I could learn anything from these faceless friends. And so, I binged as many dataviz podcasts as I could, like *Data Stories,*[5] *PolicyViz,*[6] and *Storytelling With Data.*[7]

I fell in love with dataviz, and I really wanted to start creating my own visualizations and pursue a job in the field. But I had no idea how to get there.

One evening, I was walking on the treadmill, trying to steal a few moments to myself, and as a shy introvert, a surprising thought popped into my head: *Maybe I should start my own podcast about data visualization!*

5. https://datastori.es.
6. https://policyviz.com/podcast.
7. https://www.storytellingwithdata.com/podcast.

Yes, that's it! I'd interview professional data visualization designers and ask them anything I wanted. My learning would be accelerated and anyone on the same journey could learn along with me.

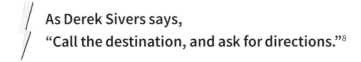 **As Derek Sivers says,**
"Call the destination, and ask for directions."[8]

One tiny problem: I'm *still* a shy introvert and listening to my own recorded voice made me want to crawl under a rock. I could hardly raise my voice loud enough to order a sandwich. How in the world would hosting a podcast work?

But, my aimlessness hurt too much *not* to give this a try. I couldn't go back to being a data analyst who crouched on the ground. This could be my ticket to a creative and fulfilling career, and the only way to find out was to act. I couldn't think my way out of this one. All that was left was a pinch of bravery.

So, I changed. I became the person who emails strangers asking for an interview, even though I was too scared to interview someone live. I'd send a questionnaire and then summarize their responses on the show by myself so I could rerecord as many times as needed (my first live interview wasn't until episode 37).

8. https://sive.rs/destdir.

It was an imperfect step to start a podcast, but it was a step.

I kept going and became the person who devours audio editing YouTube tutorials. I became the person who stays up till 3 a.m. transcribing an episode so the show notes would be up by 6 a.m. I wouldn't recommend trying that part, but I do recommend keeping the promises you make to yourself.

Since 2018, my podcast *Data Viz Today* has broadcasted almost 100 episodes, and its popularity ranks in the top 1.5 percent of all global podcasts.[9] This was my first brave step toward transforming from an order-taking data analyst into a creative data communicator with a flexible, fulfilling career.

Since starting my podcast, my creativity in the data world has flourished. I've developed comic strips explaining data literacy concepts that made people feel welcome and pursue data training. I've created dozens of infographics for businesses and books. I've designed book covers for other esteemed authors in the data visualization field, and I was invited to share my design process at Google's Measurement and Analytics conference. Throughout this journey, I've broadcast my learnings on my podcast. In

9. Listen Notes: https://www.listennotes.com/podcasts/data-viz-today-alli-torban-K4XIqSwh6rm/ Last accessed November 5, 2023.

2022, the Data Visualization Society honored me with their Impactful Community Leader award.

I've come a long way in five years. It all started when I didn't feel valued in my job, and I realized that it was partially because I was leaning on my software skills. I was only executing, not coming up with new ideas. I took one tiny, brave step and it snowballed into this career I'm proud of.

Now the tug-of-war inside of me is less intense, although I know it'll always be there. I've forged a path where I can communicate with data in creative ways, and that path comes with more freedom to choose how I spend my time, which means I get to spend more time with my kids.

I want to underscore that I've had many lucky breaks, support, and privilege throughout this journey, too. Especially when I first launched the podcast. My first couple of guests, like Lisa Charlotte Muth[10] and Nadieh Bremer,[11] generously shared their expertise with me, even though I hadn't even launched the podcast yet.

The data visualization community is so generous! If you see a particularly interesting technique or approach, send that person a message and ask if they wouldn't mind sharing how they created it. It may feel awkward, but the worst thing that can happen is that they'll ignore you.

10. Episode 01: How to Achieve Your Data Viz Goals: https://dataviztoday.com/shownotes/01.
11. Episode 02: How to Find & Represent Seasonality in Data: https://dataviztoday.com/shownotes/02.

You need to try something new to be someone new.

In summary, developing my creative practice helped me feel valued for the way I think. It's a skill that no one can take away from me. Now, if you want to change, it will take some brave steps. You'll need to go outside your comfort zone and try things that make you uncomfortable. **Embarrassment from trying new things can elevate you.**

Figure I.7: Illustration of someone comfortably standing on a rock. Next to them is someone standing taller on a rock that's held up by rocks labeled "mistakes."

Are you ready to begin your own transformation and develop your creative practice? Let's jump in together!

Summary

- You don't need to identify as a "creative type" to have creative ideas. You need to open your hands and start working.

- Creativity is the ability to generate new ideas or remix existing ones that end up being useful.

- Even if your idea is only new to you, it's still creative!

- There are four types of creative acts: mini-c, little-c, Pro-c, and Big-C. They build on each other.

- Creativity leads to innovation and moves society forward.

- To navigate creativity's pros and cons, we need a "creative practice": a set of skills and attitudes that help you generate new and useful ideas in a sustainable way.

- I found my creative practice through my career transition and starting a podcast. To find yours, it's going to take bravery to experiment and go outside your comfort zone.

Try the "So What?" prompt

Take a moment to consider what being more creative would do for you. Keep this top-of-mind to stay motivated through this journey. Here's a list to get you started, inspired by my experience and what others in the field have told me.

What would being more creative do for you?

- Stand out
- More fulfilled
- Impress clients
- Make an impact
- More self-expression

- More confidence
- Elevate quality of work
- Trust myself to find an idea
- Inspire action

Now, let's learn how to care for your creativity.

Section I
CARE

Before you dismiss the idea of caring for your creativity as vague and squishy, take a moment to recognize a potential consequence of not caring for it: **BURNOUT**.

You can relentlessly draw ideas from your creativity jar and flame out, or you can adopt a mindset and a few simple practices that will keep your creativity humming over the long haul.

The first set of tools in your creative practice will help you stay focused, confident, and refreshed during the process of generating and evaluating new ideas. They include:

- Cultivating an open frame of mind so you can recognize ideas more readily. We'll practice this with the "**Bad Gifts**" prompt.
- Strategically collect and store inspiration so you'll actually use it. We'll practice this with the "**X-RAY**" prompt.
- Building your habits to work within creativity's natural rhythm. We'll practice this with the "**Recess List**" prompt.

How I learned about creative burnout

In 2020, I created a new wallpaper design inspired by different chart types for 100 (mostly) consecutive days. I started this project to keep my hands busy at night. When COVID-19 hit, I started waking up with panic attacks and decided I had to do something else other than doomscroll in the evening. Most of the wallpapers were just alright, some were ugly little ducklings, and only a handful I proudly added to my portfolio.

Figure SI.1: Three wallpaper designs inspired by data visualization.

Despite this seemingly low success rate, the project felt like a wild success. First, it brought attention to my work, which led to new freelance projects. Second, it taught me a big lesson:

 Creativity has its own rhythm.

Here's what happened. Around day 50 of the project, I was sure that I'd cracked the creative code: I would find inputs, do some remixing, and get some cool outputs. I had optimized the creation process so that I could churn out something new every single day. I was a creative machine!

However, on day 80, burnout crept into my creative machine, grinding the gears to a halt. My mind felt like a giant brick wall. No ideas could come in, and ideas were definitely not coming out.

Figure SI.2: Illustration of a person's brain turning into a brick wall.

I had not unlocked the secret to creativity. I'd become a machine at generating creative ideas, but my machine didn't have a care and maintenance plan, so it inevitably broke down.

Creativity is a journey to find new paths, which means there will inevitably be dead-ends and roadblocks. There's no quick and efficient path to success. That's why being creative in the long run requires rest and patience. You'll have hot streaks, but you'll also have roadblocks. That's creativity's natural ebb and flow.

Todd Henry, the author of *Daily Creative*, wrote, "You can't treat your creative process (or your team's) like a machine, or you will get machine-like results: highly predictable and no more than asked. You must embrace creativity's rhythmic nature."[12] If you want a perfect circle 1,000 times over, then leave it to the machine. If you want something occasionally spectacular, then you'll need to embrace creativity's human rhythm.

Figure SI.3: Illustration of a machine stamping a circle over and over next to a free-form drawing of a flower.

 By recognizing and supporting the ups and downs of your creativity, you can get the most out of it and avoid burning out.

To do this, we'll explore three concepts in the next chapters: openness, inspiration, and habits.

12. Henry, Todd (2022). *Daily Creative.* Sourcebooks.

CHAPTER 1

Expand your mental boundaries with the "Bad Gifts" prompt

> This prompt will take your frame of mind from critical to open. It'll help you recognize the good ideas you're already having.

When a new idea pops into your head, what's the first thing you do?

In my head, I critique it. I begin a barrage of questions, like, "How would I execute that? Would that actually work? Do I have the right skills or tools? How long would it take? Won't everyone think this is a dumb idea?" This kind of critique is an essential part of creativity. After all, a creative idea is new *and* useful. But I bet you jump to critiquing too soon. You trim the tulips before they've had a chance to bloom.

Figure 1.1: Illustration of trimming a tulip bud.

We don't need to have more ideas; we need to recognize them. Meaning, don't throw your ideas out immediately. Recognize the buds you already have and give the tulip a chance to bloom.

 Suspending judgment of my ideas has been the best thing I've done to nurture my creativity.

For example, back in July 2021, I was challenged to create a blog post for the data literacy training company DataLiteracy.com that explains the pros and cons of pie charts to a general audience. It needed to bring a unique perspective and stand out from all the other pie chart articles out there. In other words, it needed to be new and useful (creative)!

Around that time, I'd been hanging out a lot in the graphic novel section of the library because my then eight-year-old daughter had a flourishing love for comics. One morning, I was sitting on a library bench, waiting for her to find a book, and a thought popped into my head: "What if I made a comic about someone trying to use a pie chart at work and it all goes wrong?"

On cue, I immediately began thinking about all the reasons that wouldn't work. I can't draw people, I don't know how to sequence a story or make interesting frames, it'll probably be cheesy and boring anyway, and I don't even read comics so how could I make one!

I wasn't just trimming this bud; I was mowing it down! I continued to sit on the bench, waiting. A few minutes later, the internal dialogue continued, "Well, I'm already in the library. I wonder if there's a book about how to draw comics…" I got up and started walking through the aisles. I quickly found an entire row of books about creating comics. I pulled down an armful and flipped through them. It turns out, creating comics is a very learnable skill! (*Aside:* if you're interested in creating comics, check out Scott McCloud's books.) I decided to give the comic a shot. I read all the books, sketched, storyboarded, and got lots of feedback.

Figure 1.2: An Illustrated Guide to Data Literacy: Pie Charts
by Alli Torban for DataLiteracy.com.

This comic was a huge success! It drove a ton of traffic to the Data Literacy site, and people were finding it useful and shareable. We can learn this information about the pie chart anywhere, but the creative way it was displayed reached people in a different way. I went on to create many more in the series tackling topics like the base rate fallacy and percent change.[13] I even got a message from someone saying that this unique style of explaining data literacy concepts finally convinced her group to pursue more data literacy training. That's a huge success, and I had almost snipped this beautiful tulip.

 I remained open a little longer than usual and gave this bud a chance to bloom.

Now, let me address a question you're likely wondering: "What if ideas don't pop in my head like that?" They do! You're probably just used to snipping them too fast to notice.

How to have more ideas

To have more ideas, you need to be more open to the ideas you're already having. At first, I found the idea of "openness" to be general and obvious, but then I found research that suggests that it's quite meaningful.

13. Read the whole series: https://dataliteracy.com/tag/comic.

The research study "The Creative Life: A Daily Diary Study of Creativity, Affect, and Well-Being in Creative Individuals" by Kaile Smith and others[14] sought to understand the relationship between personality, well-being, and creative activities. They recruited 290 creative individuals, such as early career scientists, artists with decades of experience, and hobbyists working on their passions after work, and asked them to self-assess their personality traits along with filling out a daily survey for two weeks. The survey asked how creative they were that day, whether personally or at work, and to rate their feelings, which ranged from positive to negative (e.g., energetic, happy, relaxed, sad, anxious, angry).

 They found that the strongest personality predictors of creativity were openness to experience and conscientiousness (i.e., feeling dutiful).

This mirrored my experience as well. Like in the comic example, I could see that being more open to experiences and thoughts has supported my ability to be more creative. If you want more ideas, then it's time to practice being more open in your daily life.

---

14. Kaile Smith, Alan Pickering & Joydeep Bhattacharya (2022). "The Creative Life: A Daily Diary Study of Creativity, Affect, and Well-Being in Creative Individuals," *Creativity Research Journal*, 34:4, 460–479, DOI: 10.1080/10400419.2022.2122371.

A prompt to practice your openness

Being more open seems like a passive activity, but here's a game you can play to practice. It's called "Bad Gifts" and is a classic improv game that I learned from my friend Michelle Helman[15] who's a conflict resolution expert and takes improv lessons. The game is simple: pretend to give a bad gift to someone, and they need to accept the gift as if it's exactly what they wanted.

Example:
Me: Here's a wet sock from behind the washing machine.
You: Thank you! This will help me cool down after my workout.

Doesn't it feel strange to think of a universe where a wet sock would be a great gift? It's a universe where your mind is open. Openness is a mindset that you can practice! At the end of this chapter, I'll share a list of bad gifts that you can use to play by yourself. If you play it with kids, they're going to love it, likely because they're naturally open to the ridiculous.

Your attitude and mood matter, too

There's another important finding in *The Creative Life* research paper: Individuals reported more creativity when they experience more positive emotions rather than negative emotions. I've felt that way in my creative work

15. https://www.michellehelman.com.

as well. Feeling worried or sad about something in my personal life leaves me feeling unmotivated to explore and create. When I interviewed information designers on my podcast, the consistent answer to what kills their creativity was "negative feelings."

Mesa Schumacher, a science artist who creates illustrations and infographics for clients such as *National Geographic* and *Scientific American*, told me that she has a hard time feeling creative and open to ideas when she's emotionally stressed out.

"If I have a fight with my spouse or something, I really want to resolve that before I can go and be creative… I'll have moments where I feel like my teeth are clenched and my joints are all clenched up, and I think maybe I need to do something to calm down so I can get more creative headspace."

To bring herself back into a calmer state, Mesa heads outdoors for a long walk: "I do think there's something about getting out in nature that just kind of fixes your brain."[16]

Andy Kirk, an independent data visualization expert and author of *Data Visualisation: A Handbook for Data Driven Design*, also cast a vote for negativity as a creativity killer. He says, "Ultimately, annoying things that are stressing me out will always kill my creativity. And it could be low-level

16. Episode 77: What a daily practice looks like: https://dataviztoday.com/shownotes/77.

stuff. You know, I'm very aware that in my downstairs bathroom there's a radiator that's got the potential to leak, and it's just on my mind." [17]

Those small annoyances can build up and mess with your mental state. Beyond the small things, the world experienced a collective anxiousness and fear during the pandemic. Andy found that the pandemic left him creatively bankrupt in some parts of his work.

"I couldn't write articles. I couldn't write pieces for the blog. I couldn't even face the prospect to write anything in respect of a new edition of the book. Stress, anxiety, and annoyances just become so distracting and kill that spark."

Generally, it seems a positive state of mind supports openness to ideas and therefore creativity. But it's not the only path to creativity. Remember my dataviz wallpaper project was born from pandemic anxiety. Sometimes, negative emotions can be a catalyst for creativity since they can force you to step out of your comfort zone and try something new. Overall, creativity is best supported by positivity. Keep this in mind as you try to create the conditions for ideas to flow.

17. Episode 76: Creativity is a spectrum: https://datavizoday.com/shownotes/76.

Hold space for openness and positivity, but then keep going

Here's what we've learned so far: Make sure to give your ideas a chance to flourish by being more open. Practice openness and positivity with the "Bad Gifts" prompt. But then you do need to start assessing if one of your ideas is useful. Consider this creativity flow:

Figure 1.3: Illustration of the creativity flow from ideation, rest, execution, and back again.

- **Ideate:** Be positive and open. Write down your ideas, gather inspiration, have novel experiences, and reduce negativity.

- **Rest:** Take a break, compare an idea against your needs, and get feedback.

- **Execute:** Put your head down and start implementing your idea.

When you begin a project, you'll be positive and open to ideas, move into evaluating the idea, begin executing dutifully (that's when conscientiousness shows up), but then you'll inevitably hit a snag. Something won't work as you thought, and you don't know what to try next. That's when you loop back around and evaluate, collaborate, or rest. You'll see a new problem, and then ideate again, remaining positive and open.

The key is to give space to each phase. I like to delineate each phase with some sort of action to make sure I've given it a true "session" rather than rushing through this lifecycle with racing thoughts. A few ideas to mark the beginning or end of a session: coffee break, walk outside, a meeting, or change work locations.

 Do something that puts temporal or physical space in between the sections of the creativity flow.

During my interview with Mike Brondbjerg,[18] a lead information designer for the Intelligence Unit at London City Hall, he shared a personal project that beautifully moves through this creativity flow. Before the pandemic, Mike endured long train rides to work, but he used this time to create generative artwork. He shared the artwork with his friend Frederik Vanhoutte, and they called it "Creative Commuting." One of these generative art projects involved an extremely low-tech tool: dice!

18. Episode 84: How to use serendipity to fuel your experiments and innovation: https://dataviztoday.com/shownotes/84.

First, he'd define his constraints. If he rolled the number one, what would he have to draw? A triangle or a line? Which direction would it point and what color would it be? Mike had to suspend judgment for a moment while he built his legend up to six. Then he'd dutifully execute by rolling the die and drawing whatever it told him to.

This is the ultimate stress-free way to practice the creativity flow. In just a few minutes, you can practice being open, evaluate, execute, then evaluate again, and so on. There are no consequences, and you may end up with artwork that you're proud of!

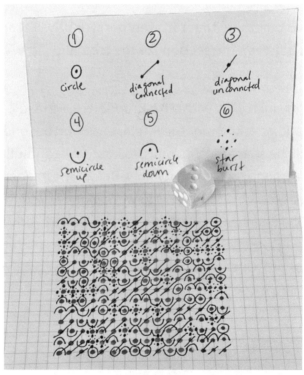

Figure 1.4: One of my generative dice artworks.

You may be wondering: "But will this really have an effect on my creativity in data communication?" Maybe, or maybe not. It may help you connect the dots in a future project. Or it may simply be an exercise in openness and serendipity.

 You can't innovate when you're always taking the most efficient route.

As for Mike, he found that participating in these "Creative Commuting" activities has helped him be more creative in his data visualization work at London City Hall. This open and iterative mindset has helped him develop creative ideas, like when he turned London census data into 3D flowers to pull readers into this data in a new way.

Summary

Here's what we learned in this chapter:

- Your idea can't flourish if you snip the bud.
- Practice being more open to the ideas you're already having.
- Openness, positivity, and conscientiousness are key ingredients to creativity, as shown in this creativity flow:

Try the "Bad Gifts" prompt

Accept these bad gifts to change your mindset to be more open:

- Here's a dusty VCR.
- Here's a gallon of spoiled milk.
- Here's an old birthday card from my grandma.

- Here's a box of expired coupons.
- Here's a rusty spoon.
- Here's a doll with missing eyes.

CHAPTER 2

Cultivate your inspiration with the "X-RAY" prompt

This prompt will take you from passively consuming inspirational work to dissecting it like a pro. It'll help you create a robust collection of inspiration that you actually use.

In my Virginia neighborhood, you can't blink twice without seeing a gray squirrel dart past. This is particularly true at my home, thanks to the majestic black walnut tree in our front yard. From my desk, I get a prime view of the frenzy as walnuts drop, drawing squirrels to crack them open and stash them all over the yard. That's the thing about a squirrel's habit of collecting nuts for winter; it's a natural instinct to prepare for leaner times. A squirrel can't wake up on the first day of winter and expect to find black walnuts still on the ground.

I can't wake up on the first day of a project and hope to be brimming with inspiration; preparation is key.

"Immature creative pros wait for inspiration.
Mature creative pros chase it down."
— Todd Henry in *Daily Creative*[19]

We need to make a habit of constantly gathering inspiration, but we often collect inspiration in a narrow way. Here are three types of inspiration we should be collecting:

- **Practical Inspiration** comes from a data visualization or infographic that solves a problem in an effective way. *Example:* you see a scatter plot in a newspaper that effectively shows a correlation between two variables, which inspires you to use a scatter plot to show a correlation in your work.

- **Internal Inspiration** comes when you're resting or doing a different task, and you have space to make your own connections. *Example*: you're wrestling with a problem, take a walk to take a break, and you suddenly realize the piece you were missing.

- **Energy Inspiration** comes from external sources not in our field that give you the spark of an idea or a bolt of energy. *Example*: you go to a museum and the superior craftsmanship in a particular exhibit gives you a bolt of energy to apply to your work.

Your inspiration can be categorized as multiple types, and the interpretation is completely up to you!

19. Henry, Todd (2022). *Daily Creative*. Sourcebooks.

Figure 2.1: Venn diagram of the three types of
inspiration: Practical, Internal, and Energy.

Do you rely on one type of inspiration more than any
others? Let's look at how you can more effectively collect
and use each type of inspiration.

Find and analyze Practical Inspiration

Collecting inspiration isn't enough. We need to analyze
it. We often look to others in our field for inspiration
because it's helpful to see how other people are innovating
in the field. However, the way we approach Practical
Inspiration often leaves us with a dusty stash and even
feeling inferior and jealous of other people's work. Have
you ever admired someone else's graphics and remarked
how talented, creative, and skilled they must be? Did you
feel like you would never get that good? I have, and I hate

feeling like that. More importantly, it's not helpful to the creative process.

That's why I developed a system for analyzing Practical Inspiration. It instantly puts me in the team mindset. We're solving problems, not competing. It also makes it more likely I'll use this inspiration in the future. The system is called "X-RAY." Whenever I see a graphic that I find particularly effective or interesting, I'll analyze it like this:

- **X:** Excited. What specifically got me excited about this graphic?

- **R:** Rules. How are they following data visualization best practices?

- **A:** Anarchy. How did they throw out the rules?

- **Y:** You. How might you use this in your own work? What are some conditions in which this would be useful?

I like to collect these in a spreadsheet so I can quickly search for keywords. Analyzing graphics also helps me remember inspirational graphics that I've seen. This is a more effective way to collect walnuts!

A note on plagiarism

Some graphics are so inspiring that it feels like a crime *not* to imitate them! But there's a fine line between being inspired and straight-up plagiarizing someone else's work. It's especially hard in data communication because no one owns a bar chart.

To make sure we don't cross the line, it's helpful to think about how a graphic is basically composed of three main elements: the data, the visual encoding, and the styling. If you pull inspiration from all of these elements and incorporate them into a single graphic, then it's going to look an awful lot like copying. It's also essential to include a note about who inspired you.

Here's another way to avoid accidentally copying too much. Once you've completed your X-RAY analysis of a graphic, put it away when you start creating your work. I've found that if I keep referencing it as I'm designing, then I'll surely end up copying more than I should.

Give your Internal Inspiration a chance to be heard

Let's say you're working on a project, making progress, and flipping through the Practical Inspiration you've gathered. But now you're stuck and not making progress anymore. This is the time to lean on Internal Inspiration. Give your brain a chance to digest and connect those dots that you've been collecting.

 Resting is a form of inspiration, too.

When you're washing the dishes, you're constantly squeezing out the sponge. Why? It's too full of soap and water to do a good job scrubbing. It's the same when your brain gets too full of information—it's not effective at solving problems anymore and you need to squeeze it out.

Figure 2.2: Illustration of a hand squeezing a sponge.

You'll hear this from professional creatives time and time again: go for a walk, take a shower, just do anything away from your work.

Neil Richards, author of *Questions in DataViz* and global data fluency lead at JLL, says that he gets the most creative ideas while on the treadmill despite his aversion to the physical activity itself. "That's almost an incentive for me to do it, thinking maybe I'll get off and I'll have another idea to scribble down and put to one side for a future project."[20]

RJ Andrews, author of *Info We Trust* and consulting data storyteller, says that he's most creative in the morning so he plans to have two focused work sessions in the morning. I asked what he does in between those sessions.

"So in between, I often exercise then because my mind is kind of like turned to mush. Like when I'm swimming in a pool, paddling on my kayak, running, or even slugging lead, then part of my brain is occupied doing the activity. It frees up the rest of it to kind of wonder and have thoughts. I think of it as free-association time, but it's time that your mind can wander. That's similar to when you're under a hot shower and you have these mental wanderings. You can achieve that without always jumping in the shower."[21]

Now that I've learned how important Internal Inspiration is to my creative work, I find myself having thoughts like, "I have so much creative work to do today, I'm going to need to take a lot of walks!" I've come to learn that taking time for Internal Inspiration is an important part of the ideation and problem-solving process.

Take the time to squeeze out your sponge so your brain can help make important connections.

20. Episode 81: Going off the beaten path: https://dataviztoday.com/shownotes/81.
21. Episode 37: How to be consistently creative. https://dataviztoday.com/shownotes/37.

Pursue new Energy Inspiration

The last part of a healthy inspiration diet is Energy Inspiration. Here, we're looking outside of our field and ourselves to find things that give us a spark of energy. This can be from creative expressions in other fields, like cinema, architecture, art, or even collaborating with other creators.

 Magical things happen when you look around your environment and fold other people's passions into your work.

In 2021, Mesa Schumacher was in the middle of a huge project called Project Animalia[22] where she'd illustrate an animal every single day for a year and post it on Twitter. I was impressed by the way she captures the beauty and detail of a wide variety of animals. At the time, I was experimenting with creating repeating patterns, and seeing her skillful work inspired me to create a pattern based on her animal illustrations. I asked Mesa if it would be OK if I used her art as a jumping-off point for a repeating pattern, and she said yes!

So, I created a fun pattern, shared it on Twitter, and to my surprise and delight, Mesa was immediately inspired to draw a piece of clothing for the same animal using my print!

22. https://twitter.com/mesabree/status/1692334068321734934.

PROJECT ANIMALIA: Day 189

Figure 2.3: Mesa Schumacher's Project Animalia Day 189:
Spotted pardalote with my pattern and her added hat.
https://x.com/mesabree/status/1413336543758929924?s=20.

We were both giddy to see each other's work and admire each other's skills. Collaborating with other people is a fun exchange of energy! Nadieh Bremer and Shirley Wu, both award-winning data visualization designers and artists, collaborated on a yearlong project where they'd each visualize a topic from a different perspective. The project pushed them both creatively and ended up as a book called *Data Sketches*. Shirley said the collaboration helped push her to use new tools, and Nadieh discovered that getting feedback from Shirley throughout the process improved her critical thinking about her work.[23]

23. Episode 61: 3 Insights from a personal project that blew up: https://dataviztoday.com/shownotes/61.

But you don't need to fully collaborate with someone on a project to get a spark of Energy Inspiration. It can be as simple as talking through your project with a friend or discussing the project with an expert. The back-and-forth is an effective tool to spark an idea or make a connection.

 The goal of Energy Inspiration is to have an experience outside your bubble and borrow some of the passion that other people have for their craft.

This can come from any field, but most commonly we find inspiration from art galleries, museums, theater, dance, concerts, music, or architecture. While interviewing Gabrielle Mérite, an accomplished information designer and data illustrator who focuses on social good, she told me that movies often inspire her. But she doesn't just watch movies, she analyzes them: "I find it really interesting to wonder how they make this mood in this specific scene? Is it the lighting? Or the angle of the camera? I take notes on movies to analyze what I like or what I respond to, and that really helped me in the long term."[24]

Gabrielle uses her notes to find patterns that she can use in her own work. She emphasizes that you should enjoy creative works but always be asking yourself: Why do I like this? Why do I specifically find this pleasing? Why do I respond emotionally to this? You can even use the X-RAY technique to analyze your Energy Inspiration. Another small

24. Episode 82: How to use your inspiration: https://dataviztoday.com/shownotes/82.

action you can take today: tell a friend about your latest project and ask them if it reminds them of anything they've seen lately.

Overall, make time to explore creations and creators outside of our field. You'll gather more tools to use and find yourself borrowing the excitement they have for their craft.

Summary

Don't wait around hoping to be inspired. Go out and actively pursue it. But it's also not enough just to collect inspiration. You need to analyze it, and make sure you're getting a balanced inspiration diet.

- **Practical Inspiration:** A spark when you see clever problem-solving in our field. X-RAY it!

- **Internal Inspiration:** A spark when you make time to let your brain rest and make connections. Squeeze the sponge!

- **Energy Inspiration:** A spark when you collaborate with someone else or explore skilled craftsmanship outside our field. Borrow their energy!

Try the "X-RAY" prompt

First, assess if you currently have a balanced inspiration diet. Which one do you need to make more time for?

To improve the way you gather and use Practical Inspiration, whenever a graphic catches your attention, X-RAY it. You can keep track of your X-RAYs in a spreadsheet or a journal. I like the former because I can search for keywords or sort.

- **X:** Excited. What specifically got me excited about this graphic?

- **R:** Rules. How are they following data visualization best practices?

- **A:** Anarchy. How did they throw out the rules?

- **Y:** You. How might you use this in your own work? What are some conditions in which this would be useful?

CHAPTER 3

Build your habits with the "Recess List" prompt

 This prompt will take you from feeling overwhelmed to focused. It'll help you find ways to persevere when you feel uninspired or stuck.

One important aspect of the creativity flow is that it's a part of a larger flow: the rhythm of your life. Sometimes you'll be moving through the creativity flow, but you're working through a tough time in your personal life. Or maybe you're just tired. You're working through a "creative winter," and that's normal and expected.

 "Creative work has seasons. Part of the work is to know which season it is, and act accordingly."
— Austin Kleon, author of *Steal Like an Artist*[25]

25. Kleon, Austin (2012). *Steal Like an Artist*. Workman Publishing Company.

Figure 3.1: Illustration of the creativity flow from ideation, rest, execution, and back again.

Figure 3.2: Illustration of the creativity flow, a part of a larger life flow with creative summers and creative winters.

As a professional, our duty persists regardless of the season we're in. The other day, a mysterious leak started dripping from upstairs right into our kitchen, so I called a plumber to find the leak. Once he came, I spent hours sprinting between floors, toggling faucets on and off, while the plumber, head buried in the ceiling gap, played detective, searching for the elusive drip. Each time I returned downstairs, he'd pop his head out with another idea ready, declaring, "Alright, well, try this..."

This reminded me of how English writer Philip Pullman responded to the idea of writer's block. He said, "Plumbers don't get plumber's block!"[26]

Being a professional with expertise means you persevere even when the solution is eluding you or you're not feeling at your best. We all have creative winters, but you must persist. In these times, focus on what you can control. This is what sets the hobbyists apart from the professionals.

When the pressure's on but I'm feeling lost in the ambiguity, I turn to habits and rituals.

Do you know who else uses habits and rituals to perform at their best? High-performance athletes. When the difference between a good athlete and a great athlete is fractions of an inch or second, then you can see why they'd turn to techniques like performing habits and rituals. You've probably noticed athletes perform simple to elaborate rituals before a game or a big shot. Basketball legend LeBron James throws chalk up into the air before the game starts. During breaks, tennis star Rafael Nadal always sips from his energy drink, then his water, and then makes sure the bottles are arranged in the exact same position on the ground.

He's so focused and precise with this ritual that it makes you wonder what's so special about those bottles! When

26. Pullman, P. (2009). Q and A's. Retrieved from https://www.philip-pullman.com/qas?searchtext=&page=4.

asked about his elaborate rituals, Nadal said, "It works for me, and they make me focus while I compete. I feel more sure of myself."[27]

In her *New York Times* article, child psychiatrist Dr. Neha Chaudhary explains that rituals serve as mental anchors for athletes, helping them prepare for unpredictable situations. We can use this tool in our lives, too.[28] Studies have shown that rituals help us improve performance by reducing anxiety,[29] regulate our emotions,[30] and give us a sense of power over the world.[31]

This is why I asked my podcast guests about their habits and rituals. Here are some of their answers:

- **Stefanie Posavec** changes her location by going to a busy cafe to sketch new ideas. The bustling sounds of other people moving, talking, and working give her the motivation and confidence to start ideating.[32]

---

27. https://youtu.be/AwgaXRAzZCo.
28. Chaudhary, N. (2020, July 6). "Rituals Keep These Athletes Grounded. They Can Help Parents, Too." *The New York Times.* https://www.nytimes.com/2020/07/06/parenting/rituals-pandemic-kids-athletes.html.
29. Brooks, Alison Wood, Julianna Schroeder, Jane Risen, Francesca Gino, Adam D. Galinsky, Michael I. Norton, and Maurice Schweitzer. "Don't Stop Believing: Rituals Improve Performance by Decreasing Anxiety." *Organizational Behavior and Human Decision Processes* 137 (November 2016): 71–85.
30. Hobson NM, Schroeder J, Risen JL, Xygalatas D, Inzlicht M. "The Psychology of Rituals: An Integrative Review and Process-Based Framework." *Pers Soc Psychol Rev.* 2018 Aug; 22 (3):260–284. doi: 10.1177/1088868317734944. Epub 2017 Nov 13. PMID: 29130838.
31. Reynolds, Celene & Erikson, Emily. (2017). "Agency, Identity, and the Emergence of Ritual Experience." *Socius: Sociological Research for a Dynamic World.* 3. 237802311771088. 10.1177/2378023117710881.
32. Episode 75: Change your space to change your mind https://dataviztoday.com/shownotes/75.

- **Andy Kirk** leans on daily routines (coffee, emails, news) to get into his workday. When he needs to transition into deep creative work, he changes his location to anywhere that gives his hands and body a different position and his eyes a different view, like a different chair in his office or traveling on a train.[33]

- **Mesa Schumacher** always starts her creative sessions with play. She allows herself to play with some color combinations or compositions without any expectations. When she's stuck, Mesa heads outside for a walk and talks herself through the problem.[34]

- **Will Chase** does a rapid round of gathering inspirational images and then starts creating and moving shapes in a design software to get his mind and body into the task. After ideating for a bit, he tries to go to sleep so he can see it with fresh eyes.[35]

- **Duncan Geere** keeps his daily habits consistent: He starts his day by sitting down at his desk and writing a list of everything he got done the previous day—both for posterity, and as a reminder to himself that he is, in fact, doing enough. During the day he takes regular breaks either to walk the dog, or just to the kitchen to get a cookie. He also has a daily ritual to gather a single piece of inspiration, which he sends out as a newsletter every ten days. This helps him process

33. Episode 76: Creativity is a spectrum https://dataviztoday.com/shownotes/76.
34. Episode 77: What daily practice looks like https://dataviztoday.com/shownotes/77.
35. Elevate Dataviz Show https://www.youtube.com/live/kU-DghqclM0.

that inspiration, and generates conversations with his
newsletter readers.[36]

- **Me:** To cue myself to begin creative work, I pour a cup
  of coffee, turn on a Hans Zimmer soundtrack, and
  light incense (the smell cues me that it's focus time!).

I've noticed that many of these habits and rituals revolve
around varying visuals, audio, or smell. To find what works
for you, try some of the suggestions here and experiment.
You may need to adjust your habits over time, too.

 **One simple habit you can start with:
Create a habit around taking a break.**

I'm terrible at taking time to rest. I want to keep working
and try to solve the problem, but the longer I work,
the more inefficient I get. Rather than waiting until I'm
completely exhausted, my habit is to decide when I'll take a
break before I begin working.

Annie Duke, a former professional poker player who won
a World Series of Poker bracelet, says that she decides
ahead of time when she's going to stop playing during a
poker match. This is because the toughest moment to quit
is when you're deeply involved, but in reality, quitting can
accelerate progress.[37]

36. Episode 78: Creativity is a risky act https://dataviztoday.com/shownotes/78.
37. Duke, Annie (2022). *Quit: The Power of Knowing When to Walk Away*. Portfolio.

So, before you sit down to either ideate or execute, decide on when you'll take a break to wring out your sponge. I know it's not realistic to take a full vacation every time you're stuck, so I've created the "Recess List" prompt. Right now, before you're in the thick of it, create some options to choose from when you need a break.

- **What can you do for a 1-minute rest break?**
  Example: Make a cup of coffee or tea, go outside to get the mail, or stand up and stretch.

- **What can you do for a 1-hour rest break?**
  Example: Take a walk, go to lunch, take a nap, read a book, call a friend, or gather black walnuts from the yard.

- **What can you do for a 1-day rest break?**
  Example: Go to the park or a museum, bake some treats and deliver them, play video games, have a movie marathon, take a long hike.

Once you have this list, start the habit of deciding when you'll take a break before you start your work. Then choose a rest activity based on how much time you have to spare. You'll begin to make a habit of quitting before you're frustrated, and you'll become addicted to the refreshing feeling of coming back to your work after wringing out your sponge!

Summary

Our creativity has seasons. Sometimes you're in a creative winter, but you're still a professional and expected to come up with ideas. Use habits and rituals to build your confidence even in uncertain times, just like athletes do. It'll take experimentation and adaptation to find what works for you. Use other people's habits as inspiration for things to try!

One of the best habits you can create is a quitting habit. Before you begin work, decide when you'll take a break.

Try the "Recess List" prompt

Make a list of resting options to choose from when you need a break to wring out your sponge:

- **What can you do for a 1-minute rest break?**

- **What can you do for a 1-hour rest break?**

- **What can you do for a 1-day rest break?**

Make it a habit to choose a time to take a break before you begin working and pick a way to rest from your list. You'll feel more refreshed, and you don't need to make any hard decisions in the moment.

Section II
COAX

"You're not blocked; you're using the wrong prompt." — Melanie Deziel, author of *Prove It*[38]

Now that we've learned a few essential elements to care for your creativity (practice being more open, cultivate a balanced inspiration diet, and develop your habits), it's time to work on coaxing out your creative ideas. To do this, I lean on prompts (i.e., questions that help bring out ideas).

Prompts are useful because they cut through procrastination and get you working on the problem. They also give you material to start shaping. Using a prompt is like overgrowing a bush so you can trim it into a beautiful topiary. Or do you remember the saying, "It's like trying to find a needle in a haystack"? To find a needle (a good idea), you first need a haystack of stuff to look through!

Figure SII.1: Illustration of a person looking through a haystack.

38. Signature Stories: Melanie Deziel (2023). *Unthinkable* podcast by Jay Acunzo. https://podcasts.apple.com/us/podcast/signature-stories-melanie-deziel/ id1094103598?i=1000625904347.

When you start brainstorming on a new project, use prompts to help you create material that you can play with and shape into a creative idea.

 Andy J. Miller, an accomplished illustrator, told me that he's found that "the most creative people are happy to play with a problem, not just try to solve it."[39]

In this section, I'll share three of my favorite prompts that help me make a productive haystack to play with.

- The "Idea Isosceles" prompt will help you stop procrastinating and gain momentum in your ideation.

- The "Break-the-Box" prompt will help you see your project through a new lens.

- The "CTR" prompt will help you find a meaningful angle in your data.

Let's go!

39. Episode 87: How to navigate the complexities of neurodivergent creativity https://dataviztoday.com/shownotes/87.

CHAPTER 4

Blast through project paralysis with the "Idea Isosceles" prompt

This prompt will take you from procrastinating to ideating in the most painless way possible. It'll help you gain momentum in your project.

Why we freeze when it's go time

Growing up in Southern Virginia, I spent countless weekend mornings practicing driving on the back roads with my dad in his red truck. We'd roll down the windows and play Hootie and the Blowfish on repeat. Everything would be great until I saw this dreaded sign:

It was time to merge onto the highway.

Figure 4.1: Illustration of a sign to merge into traffic.

The first time I tried to merge, I slowed down and searched for the perfect opening until I ran out of road.

"Stop, stop, stop … STOP!" my dad half demanded, half pleaded. Rocks pelted the bottom of the truck as I stomped the brake pedal and we skidded onto the shoulder. A dust cloud swirled around us, and I stared straight ahead with wide eyes and white knuckles.

My dad looked over and said, "Merging is harder if you slow down. There's never going to be the perfect space. Speed up, focus on the biggest space you see, and move toward it."

Still scared, I kept practicing. The next couple of merges weren't quite as dramatic. Then something unexpected happened: I had three merges in a row that were absolutely perfect. Even in heavy traffic, it felt like the sky opened and parted traffic for me. My dad dubbed me the luckiest driver on the road, and whenever we'd approach a merge, he'd say, "I bet you'll get an Alli-merge!" And I did.

The "Alli-merge" turned into a family joke to describe an inevitable lucky break. Even though it's a joke, I still merge onto the highway, fully confident that it'll be an easy merge. Is it because I'm the best driver? No. Is it because I'm really lucky? No. It's because I look for spaces instead of cars. Simon Sinek famously said, "Skiers don't think, 'Avoid the trees.' They think, 'Follow the path.'"[40]

40. https://youtu.be/W05FYkqv7hM.

Fear makes us focus on obstacles instead of open spaces. When we only see obstacles, we freeze when it's time to do the thing.

So, how do you gain the confidence to just begin and believe you'll find a creative solution? You need an on-ramp to a creative project that gives you the confidence that you'll have an "Alli-merge."

When I interviewed Manuel Canales, the Graphics Assignment Editor at *The Washington Post,* I wanted to know what he's thinking when he has a new data story to tell and he's staring at a blank page. How does he get his projects started when there are so many unknowns?

Manuel first joked that his team would look around for a "creativity button" to press. Since there isn't one, Manuel starts with just tiny doodles at the top of his page. He strings together little doodles until he finds a seed of an idea that he can develop further or talk to a colleague about.

"When starting a new project, I always recommend beginning with a paper, sketchbook, or an easy-to-discard sketch app. This is because the goal is not to put too much pressure on yourself or have any preconceived expectations. The purpose of this exercise is to explore and experiment with the data and composition to generate new ideas. Once you begin, your creativity will naturally flow," Manuel shared.

He found that the pressure to come up with a good idea extinguishes his creativity. That's why it's important to start with these no-expectation doodles as soon as possible so a looming deadline doesn't add to his stress.

What happens when these little doodles aren't surfacing any ideas? Manuel takes a break. He'll work on a different project for a bit, chat with a colleague, or try to find more inputs, like more data or design inspiration.

An "Alli-merge" for data communication

Manuel's "Alli-merge" in a creative project is to create little doodles on easily discarded paper. He's thinking, "ideas, ideas, ideas …" rather than, "nothing yet, nothing yet …"

There's no pressure, expectations, or fear. It's his time to explore some ideas that are floating around in his head. I think the magic is in the fact that he's not analyzing yet or obsessing over the brief. He's looking for a path, not for trees.

Another important aspect of Manuel's doodling is that he likes doing it. In *Do Hard Things,* Steve Magness shared research that when athletes warm up by doing what they like, they actually alter their hormonal states in a positive manner. Magness says that artists and executives can apply the same approach. When you're close to a performance, you want to prime yourself with what you like doing to get into a positive mindset.[41]

41. Magness, Steve (2022). *Do Hard Things.* HarperOne.

In my prior projects, I merged Manuel's approach of creating quick, disposable doodles with Steve's advice of beginning with what I like doing. I started with doodles of things I liked drawing, like little cubes, and then shifted into developing project concepts. It worked great, but felt disorganized. To organize this on the page, I drew a triangle and added these elements inside of it to start my ideation process. I call it…

 The "Idea Isosceles" prompt: An ideation process that helps you blast through project paralysis and find an idea to run with.

Here's how to make your own: When you start a new project, draw a triangle that fills the page with the base on the bottom and point on top. Break it into three sections.

Figure 4.2: Illustration of the Idea Isosceles, which is a triangle broken into three parts.

- **The top point is for you to draw anything that you enjoy.** It's easy to start filling this small space, and it's especially satisfying to fill in the peak! You're priming your performance by doing what you like to get into a positive mindset.

- **The middle is where you write out important parts of your brief.** I like to remind myself of the main goal of the project and the constraints I have to work within. If you don't have a good process for creating a project brief, I've added the questionnaire that I walk through with my clients to appendix A. Feel free to use it! Now we've filled most of the triangle with things we like and already know. *Can you feel the growing momentum?*

- **The base is where you start sketching concepts that might work for your project, like different chart types or compositions.** Begin drawing some concepts, either with words or visual forms, such as chart types. I like to sketch the obvious solution first to get that out of the way, and then I begin to branch out into "what-if" scenarios.

Figure 4.3: Example of an Idea Isosceles.

At the end of the Idea Isosceles, you'll likely have a seed of an idea to pursue further. Part of the magic of this prompt is that it has "idea" in its name! Believe that you'll have an idea as you move down the triangle, and you're more likely to have one. Look for a path, not the trees, and you'll get your "Alli-merge."

What if you don't have any idea worth pursuing at the bottom of the Idea Isosceles? Take a break, talk to a colleague about what you have so far, look through your X-RAY spreadsheet, and then draw another Idea Isosceles.

You'll find a seed of an idea to run with! This prompt gives you an easy way to just begin, gain momentum, and before you know it, your confidence to generate new ideas will come.

An Idea Isosceles example

Recently, in my role as a data literacy advocate at Data Literacy,[42] I was challenged with finding a creative way to teach data literacy fundamentals to an audience who isn't very comfortable with data. The training had to be fun and approachable. I had no idea where to start, so instead of procrastinating, I quickly scratched out an Idea Isosceles:

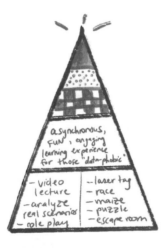

Figure 4.4: A sketch of my Idea Isosceles to find a creative idea to teach data literacy concepts.

And an idea was born! I had written "*escape room*" and thought, "That might actually work …" I pitched the idea to the team, and they loved it! So, now we're creating the very first digital escape room where the learner has to use the knowledge they've gained through the data literacy training to find their way out of the room.

42. https://dataliteracy.com.

Summary

Wait for the perfect idea and you'll run out of road, like I would when merging on the highway. You need the courage to begin, the faith that an idea will come, and then over time, your confidence in ideation will grow. Use the Idea Isosceles to gain momentum and confidence in your ideation. Now, get moving and look for the path, not the trees.

Try the "Idea Isosceles" prompt

If you're starting a new project, especially if you're avoiding it, take out a fresh piece of paper and draw a large triangle. Break it up into three sections:

- **Top section:** Draw anything you like. Make it fun!

- **Middle section:** Write keywords from your brief and your constraints.

- **Bottom section:** Start sketching and writing possible concepts. Use the left side for obvious ideas and the right side for new ideas.

CHAPTER 5

Immediately see through a new lens with the "Break-the-Box" prompt

> This prompt will take you from feeling boxed in by your assumptions to seeing a new path forward. It'll help you challenge your existing assumptions and see the problem in a new way.

One summer, a few years back, I was playing round after round of Marco Polo in the pool with my kids. One time, when I was Marco, I accidentally opened my eyes just as a tiny blackbird darted past me to scoop up a bug floating on the water. Amazed, I said to my daughters, "Wow, look at this bird!" We watched the tiny blackbird dart back and forth, from one side of the pool to the other, trying to grab its lunch. I moved toward the edge of the pool to grab my glasses and phone so I could catch it on video.

I slid my glasses onto my face, turned around, and I immediately shrieked! What I'd thought was a cute blackbird was actually a very hungry bat. We quickly jumped out of the pool and gave the bat some space to dine. The experience turned from delightful to surprising with my new lens. That's the thing about perception—it's built on our assumptions.

> **During a creative project, often the biggest roadblock to coming up with an idea is the assumptions we unknowingly hold on to.**

How a strategist challenges assumptions

On my podcast, I interviewed an accomplished strategist from the UK named Liz Hatherley.[43] We had met while collaborating on an information design project in 2022, and I saw first-hand how well she was able to challenge the assumptions that our client was holding on to. In the interview, I asked her, "How do you get a team to see past their usual assumptions and generate new ideas to solve their problem?"

First, she pointed out that if the problem is too big, then her strategy sessions with the client tend to be quiet. Liz said, "Sometimes it's good to boil everything down into just the very essential components of what it is you're trying to understand. So, rather than saying, for example,

43. https://www.linkedin.com/in/lizhatherley.

what would your idea be for a huge concept around X, Y, Z theme? Instead, it would be about saying, what one feature should we be considering? So, making things more accessible and digestible is a good way to bring people in if they're struggling to engage or come up with ideas."

Then, once Liz has helped them focus on a more specific problem, she pulls out a question that always gets the conversation flowing: What or who is our enemy?

"The idea is that you have to identify what you are rallying against with this particular piece of work. We want this work to make us better than them or their version of this. **Having an awareness of what you're trying to stand against is as important as what you're trying to stand for.**"[44]

Liz pulls out these strategies whenever a team is struggling to come up with ideas because they're stuck in the usual way of seeing the problem day in and day out. Their assumptions make it hard to see the real problem, much less any solutions. We can bring Liz's strategies into our work, too.

When you need to find a creative idea for your project, the possibilities seem endless. But consider a small part of the project first, and then the specificity will narrow down the possibilities.

44. Episode 72: How to add strategy sessions to your dataviz workflow https://dataviztoday.com/shownotes/72.

Then, identify your "enemy." This takes the pressure off what this project is and allows you to consider what it decidedly is not. After seeing how well this strategic approach worked, I tweaked it to create a simple, memorable prompt that I can do on my own, and it helps me immediately see my project through a new lens.

 The "Break-the-Box" prompt: An exercise that will help you break down a big project and challenge your assumptions.

- First, pull out a timer and draw a rectangle in the middle of a piece of paper. Then write a specific aspect of your project. Get as specific as possible. Remember, it's harder to tackle a big problem.

- Start the timer for 2 minutes, and on each side of the box, write an assumption you're making about the project.

- Then, for each assumption, write the opposite of that assumption.

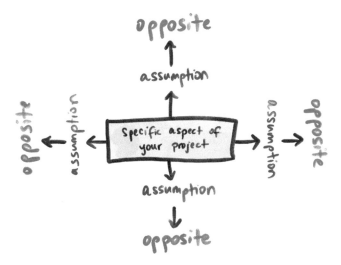

Figure 5.1: Break-the-Box prompt.

Two minutes is not much time to write all of this, and that's the point. There's no time to overthink.

A Break-the-Box example

I was commissioned by the news outlet Axios to turn research from the Harvard Kennedy School about the media manipulation lifecycle[45] into an informative and engaging infographic. I was stuck because the lifecycle was simply a series of steps in a circle. Of course a lifecycle is a circle. What else is there?

I needed to quickly push against my assumptions and see this project through a new lens. So, I pulled out my "Break-the-Box" prompt. I wrote the lifecycle in the center,

45. https://mediamanipulation.org/methods.

started the timer for 2 minutes, and wrote the assumptions I had about how this information should be displayed around each side of the box. Then I wrote the opposite of each assumption.

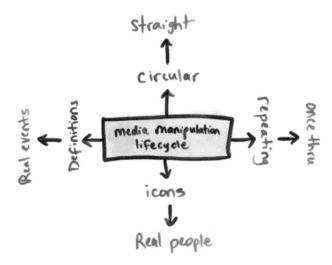

Figure 5.2: Example of the Break-the-Box prompt.

The prompt helped me see that instead of a circular lifecycle, I could try a series of events with real people. It didn't need to be circular; it's possible that a lifecycle could happen once with the rest "off-screen." Here's an early concept sketch I created after doing the Break-the-Box prompt:

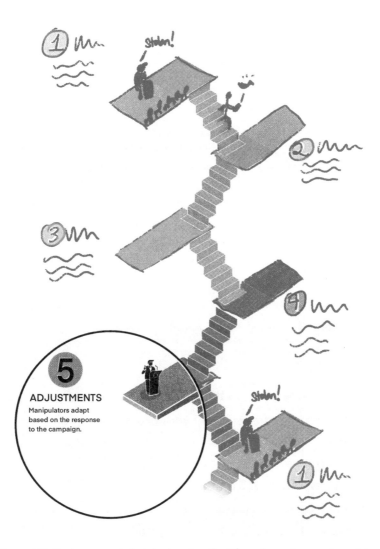

Figure 5.3: Early concept sketch showing the lifecycle as descending stairs. See the final version here: https://www.axios.com/2021/11/20/ trump-2020-election-fraud-misinformation.

This prompt broke me out of the mental box I created with my assumptions. I was able to quickly imagine other options, which led to an impactful graphic.

Summary

During a creative project, often the biggest roadblock to coming up with an idea is the assumptions we unknowingly hold on to. You can see through a new lens by breaking the project into smaller parts and considering opposites.

Next time you feel stuck in a project because it feels too big or it's hard to see a path forward, try this "Break-the-Box" prompt to challenge your assumptions and see the project through a new lens. You may just find a bat among the blackbirds!

Try the "Break-the-Box" prompt

See your project through a new lens.

- Draw a rectangle in the middle of a piece of paper.
- Write a specific aspect of your project that you're struggling with in the center of the rectangle. If that feels too challenging, write the topic or the goal of your project.
- Start a timer for 2 minutes.
- On each side of the four sides of the box, write an assumption you're making about the project.
- Then, for each assumption, write the opposite of that assumption.
- Is there an opposite that might actually offer a viable solution?

CHAPTER 6

Find stories like an editor with the "CTR" prompt

> This prompt will take your observation from obvious to meaningful. It will help you find a meaningful story in your data so people will want to read it.

The Axios graphic in the last chapter was impactful because it was meaningful to readers at that time. I didn't always understand how to pinpoint meaningfulness in a data story.

In 2017, I pitched my first data story to a local magazine about things people in my local city were google more than people in other cities. The editor called me back immediately to accept my pitch. Talking with her about the details as I finished cooking dinner, I could feel my cheeks were flush with excitement.

At that time, I'd been out of the workforce for about a year (Team Mom tugging!), and now that my youngest was one year old, I was desperately trying to find paying work that involved data that I could do from home. This pitch acceptance meant I took the leap and was flying!

But only a few hours later, the editor emailed me to ask if she could call me again. While pacing my daughter's room to lull her to sleep, the editor called just as my daughter's eyes closed. I answered with a whisper and immediately could tell something was wrong. Her voice was low and apologetic as she told me that her editor was killing the story. It was an interesting dataset, but what would anyone do with it?

I could feel my cheeks flush again, but for a different reason. I took the leap, but I wasn't flying yet. I offered no defense of the story. She was right, wasn't she? What would someone do with the interesting tidbits about Google searches by city? The story was missing something, but what? I was determined not to make this mistake again and to figure out how to create meaningful data stories.

As a data person, it's a straightforward task to find summary statistics for variables in your dataset: average, median, maximum, minimum, spread, outliers, trends, and so on. But what makes any of these numbers meaningful? Data on its own is not meaningful. Humans decide if it's meaningful or not. So how do we dig into our data to find a meaningful angle? Let's learn from the professionals who communicate information to all sorts of people every day: editors.

An editor's point of view

"The most important skill that you can have as a data visualization professional is the ability to edit yourself," Danielle Alberti told me during an interview. She's the Managing Editor of Data Visualization at Axios. Danielle went on to emphasize that you may have an exhaustive dataset at your fingertips, but it's your job to think critically about how it's going to be shaped into a relevant story.[46]

 Who decides if the story is relevant? The reader.

Marcelo Duhalde, the Associate Creative Director at the *South China Morning Post*, shared that his team is always trying to show things that are important to the readers. I asked if he thought their readers respond to their more creative visualizations because they like to see new things. He said no, what they're responding to is the relevance of the topics they cover. Even though their visualizations are creative, what truly matters to them is the subject matter and how clearly they convey the story behind it.[47]

Sahil Chinoy and Jessia Ma, both *New York Times* graphics editors at the time of my interview with them, agree on the importance of sifting through complex information and making the relevance obvious to the reader. Jessia told

46. Episode 74: What it's like being a data journalist https://dataviztoday.com/shownotes/74.
47. Episode 79: Don't exceed your audience's patience https://dataviztoday.com/shownotes/79.

me that "the story is told in the first 2 seconds."[48] These experienced editors were echoing the same sentiment that the magazine editor had communicated to me:

It's my job to quickly convey why the data is relevant to the reader. It's not enough to be interesting. The story must be meaningful.

How do you put your editor hat on and find the meaningful angle in the data?

A prompt to find relevant stories

To get more context on this question, I looked to editors outside of the data field. In *The Byline Bible,* Susan Shapiro[49] shares key considerations to make nonfiction personal short stories more meaningful to readers of newspapers and magazines. Three points from the book resonated with me: avoid the obvious, make it timely, and end in wisdom.

Applying this to data stories, I realized much of this is true for graphics that I love to read: they have conflict or tension, matter to me *now*, and make me feel like I learned something. Wanting to codify this perspective, I created a series of questions that I could run my dataset through to find angles that will likely end up being meaningful to the reader.

48. Episode 43: How to visualize paths through time with a narrative chart
   https://dataviztoday.com/shownotes/43.
49. Shapiro, Susan (2018). *The Byline Bible: Get Published in Five Weeks.* Writer's Digest Books.

The "CTR" prompt: A series of questions that will help you find a meaningful angle in your data.

- First, start with an **observation** from exploring your dataset or your topic. What have you noticed in this dataset? Is there an outlier, pattern, or relationship that's caught your attention? It's OK if it's obvious and not necessarily meaningful yet.

- Then find the **conflict**. If this is true, then what's the consequence and who is affected?

- Now, explore what makes this **timely**. Why is this important now? If it's not, what can I compare it to that is important now?

- Finally, think about possible **resolutions**. What could help? What action can we take? Where do we find more information?

Answering these questions will give you a new perspective on your data so you can frame it to be more relevant to your reader.

A CTR example

Let's see this in action by taking a seemingly dull dataset
and turning it into a meaningful story. In 2018, Makeover
Monday, the community dataviz design challenge, released
a dataset on the price of avocados over time.[50] I opened it
up and saw the prices of avocados changing over time with
extra attributes for region and whether they were organic.

My first thought was obvious. Show how these prices
change over time with a line chart and have one line for
conventional avocados and one line for organic.

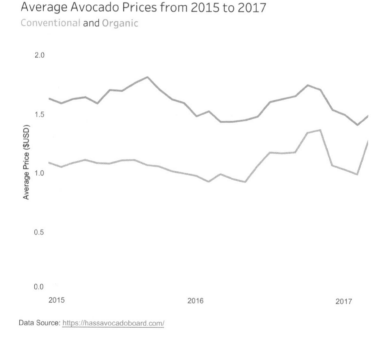

Figure 6.1: Line chart showing the avocado prices from 2015 to 2017.

50. https://www.makeovermonday.co.uk/week40-2018.

We see that organic avocados are more expensive than conventional. But we already know that. What would anyone do with that obvious information? Let's use our process to find a narrative that's more meaningful:

- **Observation:** Organic avocados are more expensive than conventional.

- **Conflict:** If organic is more expensive, then what's the consequence and who is affected? This means that some people won't be able to afford organic avocados or they'll opt for conventional avocados to save money.

- **Timely:** Why is this important now? There may be a time when organic prices come close to conventional prices, which is a good opportunity to eat organic avocados if you can't normally afford them.

- **Resolution:** What could help? What action can we take? Where do we find more information? I found that in March 2017, organic and conventional prices came the closest (about a 24-cent difference). If it were March or April 2017 right now, I could show that this is the time to grab those organic avocados and make your guacamole!

Make that guac now! Organic avocados only 24¢ more expensive
Conventional and Organic

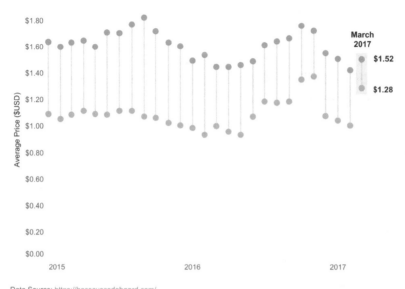

Data Source: https://hassavocadoboard.com/

Figure 6.2: Dumbbell chart highlighting the difference in
prices between organic and conventional avocados.

This is still a simple chart, but it's immediately more
meaningful to the reader than the first one because I spent
extra time framing the data using an editor's perspective.
The observation started out obvious, but we looked for the
conflict, timeliness, resolution, and came up with an angle
that someone would want to read.

This chart is also more creative because I used a dumbbell
chart to highlight the differences between the types, which
is different from the typical way of displaying this data (we
would all likely reach for a line chart).

Small changes can make a big impact on whether your chart is meaningful to your reader.

You don't need Einstein-level creativity to make a meaningful and creative data story. To help you remember this prompt, use this acronym: CTR (conflict, timeliness, resolution). By adopting the mindset of an editor, you can tease out meaningful narratives from your data to inform and inspire your reader.

Proceed with caution

This process also comes with a great deal of responsibility. It's important not to claim causation or imply relationships that can't be fully explored with the data at hand. Your graphics are a small slice of reality that is expressed through your lens. Be especially careful when your graphics support what you already believe.

For example, if you see a spike in reported crimes every Monday, could you assume that crime is highest on Mondays? Perhaps, but it could simply be a by-product of how the data was collected and reported, so the pattern doesn't merit a declaration that Mondays are dangerous. In *Data Literacy Fundamentals,*[51] author Ben Jones reminds us that there's always a gap between data and our reality. Keep that gap in mind as you interpret your data.

---

51. Jones, Ben (2020). *Data Literacy Fundamentals: Understanding the Power & Value of Data.* Data Literacy Press.

Alberto Cairo, the Knight Chair in Visual Journalism at the University of Miami, wrote in his book *How Charts Lie*, "Good charts are useful because they untangle the complexity of numbers, making them more concrete and tangible. However, charts can also lead us to spot patterns and trends that are dubious, spurious, or misleading, particularly when we pair them with the human brain's tendency to read too much into what we see and to always try to confirm what we already believe." Alberto goes on to say that a chart reveals as much as it hides.[52]

52. Cairo, Alberto (2019). *How Charts Lie: Getting Smarter about Visual Information*. W.W. Norton & Company.

Summary

Data is useless without the human lens to make meaning of it. Editors make their living creating stories that people are interested in reading, so let's learn from them! Start with your observation in the data, then identify the conflict, timeliness, and possible resolutions to uncover more meaning in your data. You may just tell a story from an angle that no one has seen before. Now that's creative!

Try the "CTR" prompt

To take an obvious observation to a meaningful data story, answer these questions:

- **OBSERVATION:** What have you noticed in this dataset? Is there an outlier, pattern, or relationship? It's OK if it's obvious.

- **CONFLICT:** If this observation is true, then what's the consequence? Who will be affected?

- **TIMELY:** Why is this important now? What can I compare it to that is important now?

- **RESOLUTION:** What could help? What action can we take? Where do we find more information?

Think about the chart type that would highlight this meaningful angle in an effective way. This will help you create a meaningful and creative graphic.

Section III
COMMUNICATE

Now that you have some tools to care for and coax out your creativity, the next set of tools in your creativity toolbox will help you shape your ideas into an effective message. In our field, we typically use data visualization or infographics.

First, do you even need a graphic to help communicate your idea?

Your idea or solution may be data-informed, but it doesn't automatically need a graphic to go along with it. Perhaps your message can be conveyed with one big number, one number compared to another, or only words. So, how do you know if you should spend time creating a graphic?

Jen Christiansen, Senior Graphics Editor at *Scientific American* and author of *Building Science Graphics,* has an extremely honed sense of when to invest time in creating a visual and when not to. Here's what she asks herself when trying to decide if it's worth creating a graphic: "Is there a piece of this story that could be told more efficiently, effectively, or completely in images rather than words? Or [consider a graphic] if there are intertwining relationships or complex processes being discussed where you need to see several things happening at the same time."[53]

53. Episode 85: How to transform science into clear and welcoming graphics https://datavivtoday.com/shownotes/85.

How to measure if a graphic is effective

Generally, we want to achieve one or more of these goals:

- **Did the graphic grab the reader's attention?**
  Perhaps we want to increase the engagement with the concept, like increasing the number of clicks on the article.

- **Does the reader understand what's happening?**
  Perhaps we want to increase the number of people who understand the concept.

- **Does the reader understand the concept quickly?**
  Perhaps we want to decrease the amount of time it takes to understand the concept.

- **Can the reader remember what they learned?**
  Perhaps we want to increase the stickiness of the concept, meaning the reader can recall important parts of the concept after a certain amount of time has passed.

It's possible to try to optimize all of these at the same time but consider this: You may be asking a single graphic to grab attention and quickly teach a concept that the reader will never forget. That's a lot of pressure on your creativity! I recommend prioritizing these goals in order of importance depending on the needs of your audience, and then tackle the top one first. For example, if you prioritize speed of understanding, then design your graphic and test your graphic on other people to prove that it's working. After that, you can pursue another goal, like experimenting with ways to grab the reader's attention.

In this section, I'll share prompts that you can use to effectively communicate your idea with your reader:

- The "4Q" prompt will help you decide how creative you should be with your ideas.

- The "Haystack" prompt will help you increase your reader's understanding of your concept by using a visual metaphor.

- The "Tango" prompt will help you discover new ways to grab attention.

CHAPTER 7

Find an appropriate balance with the "4Q" prompt

This prompt will help align any mismatched expectations between you and your client. It'll help you evaluate how far to push a project creatively.

You've likely encountered the dilemma of whether to stick to "best practices" or venture into uncharted territory with a creative approach on a project. It's a delicate balance, and it takes practice to build intuition for it. A few years ago, a client asked me to create a unique visualization to represent their survey data. It needed to show how the responses were changing over time, while also looking cool printed on a T-shirt.

Ready to please, I quickly cranked out the coolest visualization I could come up with. It was a tessellated unit chart that changed color and shape over time along with the data. Here's the prototype that I created:

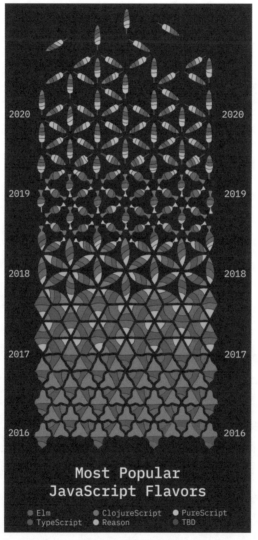

Figure 7.1: Prototype of a tessellation showing proportions change over time.

I emailed it over to my client, brimming with pride that I created something that had never been done before. *So creative!* They emailed back quickly: It wasn't what they wanted. Not even close. After I got over feeling devastated, I took this as a valuable lesson. First, logistically, time was short, but I never showed the client any sketches for feedback. A tight deadline requires heavy client interaction. Second, I didn't ask enough questions to discover how "out-of-the-box" they were expecting it to be. I interpreted "unique" and "cool on a T-shirt" to mean one thing, while they meant another. At the beginning of this project, my client and I were pointing at two different targets.

 It's my job to ask a lot of questions to make sure we get closer and closer to pointing at the same target.

Four questions to evaluate
how far to push a creative project

When you begin a new project, ask yourself four key questions. You may be able to answer these questions yourself based on past interactions with the client or the overall goals of the project; other times, the client or stakeholders need to be more involved. Plot the answer to each question on a sliding scale from 1 to 10 (low to high). Then, average the ratings, and the result will help you determine the most suitable direction for your project.

- **Q1:** How much time or patience does the reader of the graphic have?

- **Q2:** How much do I need to capture the reader's attention?

- **Q3:** How many past struggles have there been to convey this concept?

- **Q4:** How much time or resources do I, as the designer, have available?

Let's look deeper into each of these.

Q1: How much time or patience does my reader have?

Evaluate whether your reader has a lot or a little time and patience when they encounter your graphic. If your reader is pressed for time, like when you're presenting to your CEO, then prioritize intuitive and predictable visualizations.

On the other hand, if your reader has ample time to invest in decoding a novel graphic, like someone leisurely reading a magazine, then you have more leeway to experiment with a new approach.

Consider who the reader is and what's going on in their life at the time they encounter the graphic. Imagine opening the newspaper on your morning commute to quickly check the weather, and you find a novel chart trying to convey the emotion behind the amount of sunshine today. It'd be frustrating.

Marcelo Duhalde, the Associate Creative Director at the *South China Morning Post*, says that his team constantly tests their visualizations on each other, potential readers, and other journalists to make sure they aren't surpassing their reader's patience. The last thing they want is for a reader to find the visualization to be too cryptic and wish the data was in a table instead.[54]

In what situation is your reader most likely to encounter your graphic? In that setting, how much time and patience will they have to decode your graphic? Rate your answer from 1 (a little) to 10 (a lot).

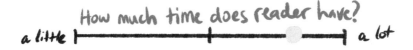

Figure 7.2: Rate how much time your reader has from a little to a lot.

When I'm close to 1, I'll focus on reducing friction for the reader by having a strong visual hierarchy (i.e., it's clear what the reader should read first, second, and third by using size, position, or color). I may also make it very obvious why this information is important to them (e.g., actionable title or highlight specific areas).

54. Episode 79: Don't exceed your audience's patience https://dataviztoday.com/shownotes/79.

When I'm close to 10, I feel more confident to try novel chart types, extra color, illustrations, incorporating stories, or adding eye-catching elements like animation.

Q2: How much do I need to capture my reader's attention?

Next, consider if you need to grab your reader's attention. In situations where you have a motivated audience who needs the information concisely, stick to clear and straightforward graphics. They don't need to be enticed into the subject matter; they just need the information.

However, if capturing attention is crucial, such as in social media campaigns or magazine articles, try incorporating unique and engaging elements to draw the reader in, what Jen Christiansen calls a "welcoming gesture." That could include extra illustrations or stories that indicate to a reader that this topic is for them.

"I love a good minimalist diagram as much as the next person, but sometimes they feel a little bit cold. So how can you draw somebody in? One way to do that would be with illustrative details to make that abstract topic more relatable, like a small drawing of the object or subject matter of the graphic. Or using visual metaphors that can provide immediate context," Jen explains.

Of course, we always want our reader to feel welcome when reading our graphics, but that doesn't mean every graphic needs a welcoming gesture. It depends on the context. "I wouldn't necessarily want my accountant or my doctors to be putting in little illustrations into the charts about my blood work," Jen continues. "Would a welcoming gesture be useful in that case, or will it be a distraction?"[55]

It's not always clear whether you need a welcoming gesture or not but consider the time and place the reader will encounter the graphic. Would extra elements overwhelm the information that you're trying to share? Or will it draw the reader into the topic?

Ask yourself, how attentive and interested is my reader in this topic? Do I need to grab their attention to pull them into this information? Rate your answer from 1 (a little) to 10 (a lot).

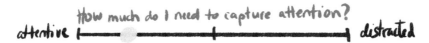

Figure 7.3: Rate how much you need to capture your reader's attention.

When I'm closer to 1, I'll focus on reducing the reader's friction to get the information they need. Just like when someone is low on time, this person is typically searching for a particular answer and any extra elements are a distraction. We should strive to deliver what they expect to see. However, they could be attentive but are expecting to be entertained. So they may score low on this question

55. Episode 85: How to transform science into clear and welcoming graphics
https://dataviztoday.com/shownotes/85.

but high on the previous question because they have more time. That's why we ask four questions and then average your responses to make the final decision.

When I'm closer to 10, I'll reach for a "welcoming gesture" typically in the form of an illustration or story. I may also try novel chart types, extra color, illustrations, or adding eye-catching elements like animation.

Q3: How many past struggles have there been to convey this concept?

Assess if there have been difficulties in conveying the concept in the past. If there haven't been any issues, it's best not to deviate from what works. Conversely, if the concept has been challenging to communicate, try a fresh approach, like incorporating a visual metaphor.

Ask yourself, have there been a lot of struggles to convey this concept in the past? Are readers consistently confused with the way this information is presented? Rate your answer from 1 (no confusion) to 10 (lots of confusion).

Figure 7.4: Rate how many struggles there have been to convey this concept in the past.

When I'm closer to a 1, I'll tend to stick with best practices and what's already working. I won't risk adding confusion by trying something new. However, when I'm closer to a 10, that's an opportunity to try something new since the "old way" is obviously not working.

Q4: How much time or resources do I have available?

Finally, consider your constraints. Do you have a lot of time? Do you have a lot of money to buy materials or technologies? With limited time or access to resources, stick to tried-and-true methods. However, if you have an abundance of resources, then experiment and explore new ways to present your ideas. Rate your answer from 1 (a little) to 10 (a lot).

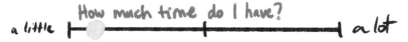

Figure 7.5: Rate how much time or resources you have as the designer.

By now, you probably have a general feeling about how far you should push this project creatively, but if you're not sure, then add up your ratings across all four questions and divide by four to get the average. If the average is under 5, then do what you know works. Anything over 5, this is likely a good time to use your resources to experiment with new ideas.

Don't forget about yourself

Trying something new and presenting it to a client or reader can end in a lot of different ways, good and bad. Your idea may be welcomed with cheers, accolades, and promotion! Or it might be met with skepticism, and you feel embarrassed. Or you may even lose the project or client, which can strain your finances and personal life.

Creativity is risky. Duncan Geere, an information designer living in Sweden, brought up this point during my interview with him. He said, "For me, the consequences of a project and experiment not working out are really low. They're much lower than they might be for somebody who has huge debts, or a disability of some kind, or a family to feed, or all kinds of reasons that have nothing whatsoever to do with that person's talents or their abilities."[56]

Not only does a person's home life impact their ability to risk being creative, the place they live matters too. Some countries or states do not welcome those expressing themselves outside of the norm. This chapter is called "find an appropriate balance," and I mean for you, too. There is risk in creativity and you're right to listen to that inner voice that sometimes whispers, "It's not worth the risk right now." I want you to push yourself and create innovative work and happy clients, but you also need to take care of yourself.

56. Episode 78: Creativity is a risky act https://dataviztoday.com/shownotes/78.

Summary

Working with clients and stakeholders is tough because you both enter the project with different expectations and goals. It's your job to make sure you're both pointing at the same target and setting expectations for how "new and creative" the solution is.

Ask questions to assess whether this is a good situation to just go with best practices or if you should push for something new. Does your reader have time, patience, attentiveness, understanding? Do you have a lot of time? No two situations are the same. Also, keep in mind that creativity is a risky act, so take care of yourself.

Try the "4Q" prompt

When you begin a new project, ask yourself or your client these four questions and plot the answer on a sliding scale from 1 to 10 (low to high). Then, average the ratings and the result will help you determine the most suitable direction for your project. Less than 5, then stick with the "tried-and-true" solutions. More than 5, this may be a good time to experiment!

- How much time or patience does the reader have?
- How much do I need to capture the reader's attention?
- How many past struggles have there been to convey this concept?
- How much time or resources do I, as the designer, have available?

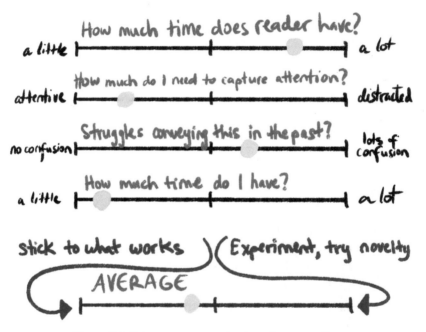

Figure 7.6: Rate your answers to these four questions.

CHAPTER 8

Explain it using a visual metaphor with the "Haystack" prompt

> This prompt will help you take your reader from confused to enlightened. It'll help you find a visual metaphor to explain your concept in a new way.

Now that you've learned to calibrate how creative you can be in your project, let's see how visual metaphors can increase your reader's understanding and the memorability of your concept.

When I began studying data visualization, I noticed that there was a type of graphic that seemed to stand apart from the rest. It had this extra layer of emotion and seemed to explain a complicated idea effortlessly. I finally put my finger on this X factor when I interviewed Valentina

D'Efilippo on my podcast.[57] As a personal project, she created a scatter plot about the duration and number of lives lost in wars around the world, but she went beyond choosing a standard chart type for the data.

Valentina wanted to humanize this data. She thought about how the poppy flower is used as a commemorative symbol for lives lost in war, and she realized that she could turn the scatter plot into a field of poppies. It would be a data-driven field of commemoration where, instead of using traditional dots, she used poppy flowers. The resulting graphic was published in a book, won an Information is Beautiful Award, and was shared widely by people in and out of the data visualization field.

One reason this graphic was so successful is that Valentina took the time to wrap the data with an extra layer of humanity by using the poppy field as a visual metaphor. This evoked emotion from her readers and made it more impactful and memorable.

In this chapter, you'll learn what a visual metaphor is, when to use it, and my handy prompt to create your own.

57. Episode 14: How to use visual metaphor to evoke emotion
https://dataviztoday.com/shownotes/14.

What's a metaphor?

The word metaphor comes from the phrase "to transfer."[58] We transfer our knowledge of one thing to another. The metaphor suggests a point of similarity between two things. For example, in a hot room, I might say, "This room is a sauna!" You know that I don't actually think we're in a bathhouse in Finland. You understand this to mean, "This room is so hot, it feels like we're in a sauna!" Since you already know a sauna is a hot room, your mind transfers that similarity to the current situation.

A metaphor also adds another layer of information to our communication. In the sauna metaphor, you understand that the temperature is too high, *plus* you might see an image in your mind of someone sweating profusely in a dark room. Or you might remember that time you were in a sauna and passed out!

That's the power of metaphor, and we use metaphors so much that we don't realize we're doing it! Did you catch the metaphor in the last paragraph? I said that metaphor adds a layer of information. I'm using the metaphor of something that has layers, like a tiered cake, to explain the benefit of metaphor.

So, what's a **visual** metaphor? It's when we use visual cues to convey the metaphor, like when Valentina added images

58. *Etymonline Dictionary.* Date accessed Nov. 8, 2023.
https://www.etymonline.com/word/metaphor.

of poppy flowers to her graphic. When we use a visual metaphor, we can seamlessly transfer information and trigger extra emotions, just as we use metaphors when we write and speak.

In 2022, I helped researchers Eli Holder and Cindy Xiong explain their research about the potential harm that bar charts can cause when used to display demographic data.[59] **I used the metaphor of an optic diagram to help create this infographic:**

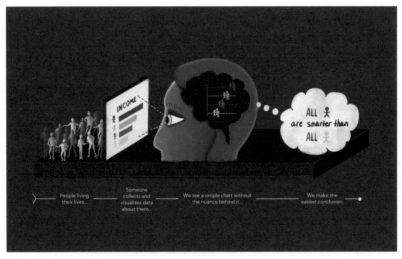

Figure 8.1: Illustration of how people perceive bar charts and make assumptions about the people behind them.

As I share my process for finding a visual metaphor in this chapter, I'll use this infographic as an example so you can see the messy brainstorming process behind the final piece.

59. E. Holder and C. Xiong, "Dispersion vs Disparity: Hiding Variability Can Encourage Stereotyping When Visualizing Social Outcomes," in *IEEE Transactions on Visualization and Computer Graphics,* vol. 29, no. 1, pp. 624–634, Jan. 2023, doi: 10.1109/TVCG.2022.3209377.

Visual metaphor is an extremely powerful tool in our creative practice. The hard part is coming up with a visual metaphor that's right for your project. But even before that, part of your job is to determine if a visual metaphor is needed at all.

When's a visual metaphor useful?

I've learned to listen for key concerns from my client that prompt me to explore using a visual metaphor:

1. "We've tried to explain this many times before, but our reader just doesn't get it."

2. "We want our audience to feel a certain emotion."

3. "We want our readers to be able to remember what they learned and share it with others."

These concerns speak directly to the strengths of visual metaphors because they …

1. Use our understanding of something else to help us grasp something new.

2. Evoke images and memories, which often trigger emotions.

3. Make the idea more memorable with its novelty and personal associations.

So, how do you create one? Through research and trial and error, I've developed a brainstorming process to create my own visual metaphors. Keep in mind that this is a hard skill to learn. Don't be frustrated with yourself the first time you try to generate a visual metaphor. The creative process is messy, and this is no exception.

My process for developing a visual metaphor

The goal of this process is to find the source of our metaphor. Then we can identify parts of the source that we can transfer onto our concept.

STEP 1: Write a summary sentence of what you're trying to communicate. This means that you need a strong understanding of what you're trying to convey. You may need to work with an expert in that field.

- *Example:* Researchers Eli Holder and Cindy Xiong wanted to present their research at IEEE Vis 2022. They had found that bar charts showing data about demographic groups tend to oversimplify trends; they highlight the differences between groups while failing to account for nuances within each group. This perpetuates stereotypes about the people in that demographic. But their reviewers commented that their diagrams trying to show this were confusing. Since they were so deep into the research, they were unsure how else to explain their idea. Hearing this, I knew it was my clue to explore a visual metaphor.

Together, we developed this summary sentence: Bar charts make personal attribution easy because they exaggerate between-group differences and downplay within-group variability.

STEP 2: Answer a set of brainstorming questions. These questions are meant to help you gather more details about the concept so you have something to work with. This is all part of creating a haystack that we can look through in the next steps.

Think about the attributes (i.e., features or traits) of the thing you're trying to convey, and answer these questions:

- What are the notable features of your concept?
  - *Example:* Bar charts are influential on someone's opinion of another group. They can hide nuance.

- What's the purpose or value of those features?
  - *Example:* The purpose of being influential is to change someone's mind. The purpose of hiding nuance is to make decisions easier.

- How are the features arranged, structured, or related to each other?
  - *Example:* Being influential often means simplifying information so more people can understand it, which often leads to hiding nuance. One might come before the other.

- Is there a glue holding it all together?
  - *Example:* Someone is shaping a message and someone is perceiving a message.

Also, think about the process or transformation that happens in your concept, and answer these questions:

- What's the beginning state like?
  - *Example:* A bar chart is created by someone collecting data on a group of people.

- What's the transformative action?
  - *Example:* Other people see that chart without a full understanding of the original data.

- What's the ending state like?
  - *Example:* The person makes assumptions about the group.

- What's the overall effect?
  - *Example:* A bar chart may be perpetuating a stereotype.

STEP 3: Pick out keywords in the answers you wrote down in steps 1 and 2. These are words that are integral to understanding the idea. Usually, these are nouns and verbs. I also circle anything that conjures an image in my mind.

- *Example:* Bar charts make personal <u>attribution</u> easy because they <u>exaggerate</u> between-group <u>differences</u>

and <u>downplay</u> within-group <u>variability</u>. Bar charts are <u>influential</u> on someone's opinion of another group. It can <u>hide</u> nuance. The purpose of being influential is to <u>change</u> someone's <u>mind</u>. The purpose of hiding nuance is to make decisions easier. Being influential often means <u>simplifying</u> information so more people can understand it, which often leads to hiding nuance. One might come before the other. Someone is <u>shaping</u> a message and someone is <u>perceiving</u> a message. A bar chart is created by someone <u>collecting</u> data on a group of people. Other people <u>see</u> that chart without a full understanding of the original data. The person makes <u>assumptions</u> about the group. A bar chart may be <u>perpetuating</u> a <u>stereotype</u>.

STEP 4: Write down synonyms, antonyms, or images that come to mind for your keywords. I rewrite the keywords in a list and use an online thesaurus to look up related words.

- *Example:*
  - Attribution – assign, cognition, classify, category, judge, evaluate
  - Exaggerate – overdo, hyperbole, magnify, overestimate
  - Differences – unlike, separate, distinguish
  - Downplay – wave off, trivialize, understate, minimize
  - Variability – change, uneven, alter, varicolored
  - Collect – grouping, collate, gather
  - Assumption – presume, hypothesis, theory

- ○ Perpetuate – mummify, prolong, eternal
- ○ Stereotype – classify, pigeonhole, sort

STEP 5: Pick out keywords again, grabbing words that would apply to different categories or genres, and list out those associations. For example, above I wrote "judge" as a synonym for attribution, which makes me think of a judge in a courtroom or a referee at a sports game. This step is important because our goal is to lean on our reader's understanding of something else in order to explain our concept.

- *Example:* Here are words from the previous step that remind me of other categories: classify (biology), judge (law), magnify (physics), witness (law), pigeonhole (career). Going further:
  - ○ Classify – kingdom, animal, insect, rocks, gems, shapes
  - ○ Judge – court, gavel, referee
  - ○ Magnify – zoom in, lens, magnifying glass, optics, microscope
  - ○ Witness – court, religion
  - ○ Pigeonhole – business, school, birds

STEP 6: Sketch a few ideas that sparked a connection with your concept. By now, there are usually one or two words that stick out as having some similarities or points of connection with your concept. Pull those words out and start sketching how this source would map onto your concept. Do they have similar attributes? Do they have the same goal or use?

- *Example:* The word that stuck out to me is **optics** (under magnify). It reminded me of an optic diagram from school when they taught how lenses work.

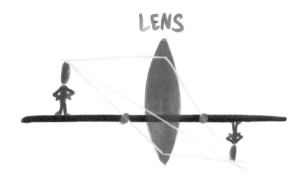

Figure 8.2: Sketch of an object being refracted through a lens.

I could see the similarities to the concept I was trying to explain for Eli and Cindy. There was someone looking at a bar chart (the lens) that was distorting the view of people living their lives. Then the person perceives the situation differently than it actually is and stereotypes certain people. Here's how I mapped the optic diagram (the metaphor source) onto my concept (the target):

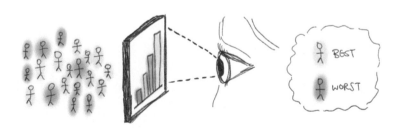

Figure 8.3: Sketch of the infographic for Eli and Cindy, leaning on the optic diagram metaphor.

STEP 7: Test your sketches. Ask someone else what they think your sketch is trying to convey. You will inevitably lose some of the nuance in your concept by using a visual metaphor. Losing *some* nuance is OK, but if your reader misses the point or they're even more confused, then you'll have to adjust. Also, don't overload the metaphor. It's tempting to extend the metaphor as far as possible, adding all sorts of detail, but you risk making it harder to understand or even misleading.

- *Example:* I presented this sketch to Eli and Cindy, and they pointed out a bit of nuance that the sketch lost during the cognition process inside someone's head. I revised the sketch to make this part of the cognition process more clear and tested it on a group of 20 testers from the website usabilityhub.com. Even with no context, 15 out of 20 readers (75%) were on the right track in understanding why bar charts could be problematic when representing data about groups of people. This is a huge improvement on Eli and Cindy's original image, which resulted in 6 out of 20 (30%) testers on the right track.

Summary

Visual metaphors help our reader understand complex topics by leaning on information they already know. They also add another layer of emotion and memorability. Reach for a visual metaphor if your client is concerned that their concept is too complicated for their reader, it's lacking emotion, or it's important for the reader to remember the information. To find a visual metaphor, you need to find a source that you can map your concept onto. It's a messy process, but the steps that I shared with you will help create a productive haystack in which to find your needle!

Try the "Haystack" prompt

Follow these steps to brainstorm a visual metaphor:

- **Step 1:** Write a summary sentence of what you're trying to communicate.
- **Step 2:** Answer these questions to start building your haystack: What are the notable features of your concept? What's the purpose or value of those features? How are the features arranged, structured, related to each other? Is there glue holding it all together? What's the beginning state like? What's the transformative action? What's the ending state like? What's the overall effect?
- **Step 3:** Pick out keywords in the answers you wrote down in steps 1 and 2.
- **Step 4:** Write down synonyms, antonyms, or images that come to mind for your keywords.
- **Step 5:** Pick out keywords again, grabbing words that would apply to different categories or genres, and list out those associations.

- **Step 6:** Sketch a few ideas that sparked a connection with your concept.
- **Step 7:** Test your sketches and adjust.

CHAPTER 9

Mix different mediums and experiences with the "Tango" prompt

 This prompt will help you generate more interesting ways to share your concept. It'll help you quickly mix and match elements to generate new ideas.

A creative idea doesn't need to be completely new. It can be a remix of things that already exist. In this chapter, I'll share a few examples of remixing that communicates information in a unique way. Then I'll give you the tools to mix and match ideas yourself or with the help of artificial intelligence (like an AI chatbot).

Mixing data, music, and podcasts

Duncan Geere, the information designer specializing in climate change based in Sweden, and Miriam Quick, a data journalist based in the UK, recently teamed up to create a podcast called *Loud Numbers.*[60]

 Through the podcast medium, they bring together data and music to communicate data stories.

One episode is called *The End of the Road,* which is a requiem for lost biodiversity, driven by a sonification of data on insect population decline. Duncan and Miriam put data into music to create a unique way to understand the declining insect population. Here's how they describe the track: "You can hear two layers of data encoded in the music. The number of insects splattered onto Møller's car each month is represented by the number of fluttering synth sounds in a bar. Higher sounds represent smaller insects, while lower sounds correspond to larger insects. As the number of insects falls, the sounds fall silent and the track empties out … There are ambient sound effects— cars zooming past, birds singing. There's a sparse texture that gets even sparser as the insects disappear over time. Finally, there's a funeral bell that tolls for every year that passes in the dataset."

Duncan explained more during our interview, "It's a lot of fun, but the creative combination there is basically just sonification plus podcast, which it turns out that no one had ever combined before. So, you know, boom— creativity!"

60. Loud Numbers podcast https://www.loudnumbers.net.

Mixing data, experience, and books

Here's another creative mix with Miriam Quick, but this time she teamed up with Stefanie Posavec. They collaborated on a book called *I am a book, I am a portal to the universe,*[61] which gives readers the chance to experience data.

> **Through the book medium, they bring together data with time, touch, and experience to share the wonders of the physical world.**

Miriam says, "We wanted to create a book where everything was on a one-to-one scale. And the data, because we always work with data together, the data would be embedded, not just printed on the page, but actually embedded in the book itself and encoded using all the dimensions of the book. So, its weight, length, area, volume: all these different kinds of physical variables that emerge from the book design process itself."[62]

Stefanie and Miriam brought together data about the world and embedded it into the book. You can hold your finger up to a page and see how long your nails will grow over two years, or in the time it took you to read a particular sentence, discover what would have just happened in the world during the time that's passed.

61. S. Posavec and M. Quick (2021). *I Am a Book. I Am a Portal to the Universe.* Particular Books. https://www.iamabook.online.
62. Episode 58: How to turn data into an experience https://dataviztoday.com/shownotes/58.

This new way of experiencing a book is immensely creative and has brought wonder to so many people! It even won the Royal Society Young People's Book Prize in 2021.

Mixing data and comics

Remember my comic series back in chapter 1? I was looking for a way to explain data literacy concepts in a new way and was inspired to create a comic series after watching my daughter enjoy her comic books so much.

 Through the comic medium, I brought together data literacy and humor to teach data concepts.

Using the comic format is not a common way to understand data concepts, which is why it's so effective! Sometimes a new format extends your reach to people you wouldn't normally have access to. I received a message from someone who said my comic was a "softer" way to explain data concepts and really resonated with her and her team. So much so, she decided to pursue more data literacy training!

Mix and match elements from these lists to find a creative way to communicate your idea

Take the concept you're trying to communicate and combine it with elements from the following lists as a thought experiment. Imagine what it would look like if these elements were brought together. I call this prompt "Tango" because we pair up different elements from these lists, they dance together for a moment, and we decide if they should partner up.

First, pick an item from the *mediums* list and an item from the *experiences* list.

Mediums

- Paint
- Sculpture
- Collage
- Textile
- Newspaper
- Magazine
- Comics

- Article
- Book
- Infographic
- Digital art
- Photography
- Video
- Blog

- Social media
- Podcast
- Radio
- TV show
- Exhibit

Experiences

- Taste
- Smell
- Visual
  - Brightness
  - Color
  - Contrast
  - Depth
  - Motion
  - Shadow
  - Blur

- Sound
  - Rhythm
  - Vibration
  - Loudness
  - Pitch
  - Tempo
  - Timbre
- Touch
  - Temperature
  - Pressure

  - Texture
  - Pain
  - Wetness
- Time
  - Duration
  - Movement
  - Pace
  - Frequency
  - Delay

Now, fill in this sentence with the elements you chose:

Through the _____ medium, I brought together _____ experience and _____ concept (your concept).

You don't need to fit the sentence exactly. Here are a couple of examples:

1. Through the sculpture medium, I brought together the experience of touch and someone's career data by creating an art exhibit.

2. Through the textile medium, I brought together the time it takes for various materials to decompose and the time it takes me to knit a certain section of a blanket.

If you'd like to generate variations of these sentences more quickly, here's a prompt you can put into an AI chatbot: **"My concept is <explain your concept, the data you have or challenge you're trying to solve>. Use the lists of mediums and experiences below to generate 100 variations of mediums and experiences and how they can apply to my concept."** Paste in this prompt and the lists of Mediums and Experiences from the previous page, and you'll soon be swimming in Tangos!

Most of them won't make much sense, and that's OK. This is a thought experiment to think of something someone has never thought of before. Here's one that I tried: "My concept is wanting to use data to make people interested in going to the library more often. Use the lists of *mediums* and *experiences* below to generate 100 variations of mediums and experiences and how they can apply to my concept."

These are a few ideas that I thought had potential:

- An **exhibit** that integrates **pace**, showing the speed at which different books are read or returned.

- **Digital art** installations that use **sound** patterns or **rhythms** to represent popular library genres.

- **Social media** posts that invite users to share the **texture** of their favorite library books.

Summary

A creative idea doesn't have to be completely new; it can be a remix of existing ideas. This takes the pressure off of coming up with a creative idea. The more elements you bring into your work, the more unique it'll be!

Try the "Tango" prompt

What are you working on right now? What would it look like in a different medium? What could you do to incorporate another experience around it? By giving the elements from these lists a chance to "dance" together for a moment, we can quickly generate new ideas. Use the lists in this chapter to fill out variations of this sentence:

Through the _____ medium, I brought together _____ experience and _____ concept (your concept).

Or use this prompt in an AI chatbot: **"My concept is <explain your concept, the data you have or challenge you're trying to solve>. Use the lists of mediums and experiences below to generate 100 variations of mediums and experiences and how they can apply to my concept."**

Conclusion

Here we are at the end, but it's really the beginning, isn't it?

Do you remember, just a handful of chapters ago, you felt frustrated that creative ideas were saved for the "creative types," or worse, only happened if you were lucky? We discovered that the problem is passively waiting for inspiration to hit and we're capable of enabling our own creativity. With the prompts I've provided, you're empowered to dive into your creative work with confidence.

I hope you've remained open as I shared a new perception of creativity, one where you don't need to be a creative genius. I hope you'll be daring enough to engage with these prompts, and that you find the confidence to let your tulips blossom.

MY ONE LAST PIECE OF ADVICE:
Creating and sharing new ideas is hard work.
Try to separate your personal sense of value from
the value of your idea. They're different. Your value
is inherent. The value of your idea is subjective,
and it'll take a lot of iteration to find a keeper.

As you close this book, please keep moving. The journey of creativity is not about reaching a destination. Once you leave the land of passivity, you're on the path to creating work that makes you stand out and innovate. So, here's to you, the creative force you've always been. Here's to getting your hands dirty and creating something remarkable, something uniquely you.

Here's to all your future chart sparks.

What to do next

Right now, how do you feel?

- **Energized:** If you have a project to work on, revisit chapter 4 about the "Idea Isosceles" and start brainstorming! If you don't have a project right now, revisit chapter 6 about finding meaningful stories and use it to start a personal project that's important to you.

- **Overwhelmed:** Revisit chapter 2 about cultivating your inspiration. Buy a newspaper and X-RAY every chart or infographic you see. Scribble in the margins, cut them out, and make a mess!

- **Inspired, but lonely:** If you're on the go, give podcasts a try: *Data Viz Today, Elevate Dataviz Show, Explore Explain, Loud Numbers, The Data Journalism Podcast, Data Stories, PolicyViz, Storytelling with Data, Present Beyond Measure Show,* and *Data Plus Love* (to name a few!). It's astounding how close you can feel to someone by listening to their voice. Also, revisit chapter 2 about Energy Inspiration, and reach out to someone whose passion for their craft really inspires you. Tell them what you love about their work, and see what happens. I'd also recommend joining communities to connect with others going along the same journey, like the one I cofounded, the *Elevate Dataviz Learning Community*. The *Data Visualization Society* also has lots of resources and an active community!

Acknowledgments

First, thank you to my husband, Steve. We make a great team, and I love you. Thank you to my daughters, Eva and Anna, who are always excited to weigh in on new designs. Your enthusiasm for my work keeps me motivated. Thank you to my mom, Linda, who believes in me more than I believe in myself.

This book wouldn't be here without a lot of support and pep talks from my friends and colleagues. Thank you to the Data Literacy team—Ben Jones, Becky Jones, and Megan Hanno—for your guidance and support in making this book everything I hoped it would be and more!

Thank you to my mentor, Steve Wexler, who pushed me in the kindest way to get my book proposal done and sent out, even when I had epic self-doubt.

Thank you to the entire Elevate Dataviz Community, especially Duncan Geere, Gabrielle Mérite, Will Chase, Sonja Kuijpers, Ben Oldenburg, Jane Zhang, and Gurman Bhatia, for your friendship, support, and advice.

Thank you to Alberto Cairo, Tamara Munzner, and Amanda Makulec who gave me early thoughts on the book and cheered me on, giving me the confidence to go for it.

Thank you to all my devoted beta readers who waded through my repetitive, cloudy thoughts and helped me turn this into a clear and succinct book: Amanda Alley, Kat Greenbrook, Alyssa Cropley, Brianna Wilson, Maggie Shi, Maxene Graze, Zan Armstrong, Mark Bradbourne, Sara Stoudt, Kassie Scott, Jerilyn Libby, Schubert de Abreu.

Thank you to Lorie DeWorken for using your creativity to make this look like a beautiful book!

A final huge thank you to everyone I've interviewed on the podcast. You've generously shared your wisdom with me and helped create who I am today. Also, thank you to everyone who listens to the podcast! I love receiving your messages that share your breakthroughs and career wins. It's an honor to be a small part of your dataviz journey.♥

Appendix A

Use my data communication project questionnaire below before you begin a project. It will help you and your client point at the same target, and give you clear guidelines to reference as you're creating.

PROJECT CONSULTATION

Project Details

- What is the project?
- Why are you doing this project?
- Why are you doing this project now?
- What is your timeline?
    - Are there intermediate deadlines?
- What is your goal for the project?
- How will we know that we're successful? What will be different from what's happening now?
    - How can we measure that? Is there a leading indicator?
- How will we know we're not successful? What would have happened for this project to be a failure?

- What challenges do you foresee with this project?
- Are there any absent stakeholders we need to keep in the loop?
  - Who needs to approve the final graphic?
  - Who will handle other implementation components? (development, etc.)

Audience

- Who is this project for?
  - What are a few words that describe your audience?
  - What are they struggling with?
  - How interested are they in this topic?
  - How attentive will they be when they meet the graphic?
- What's our promise to our audience?
  - After they see this project, they'll know …
  - After they see this project, they'll have …
  - After they see this project, they'll be able to do …
  - After they see this project, they'll feel …
- Can we measure any of those promises?
- Assumption check: What indication do you have that they want any of those things?
- What's at risk if your audience doesn't receive your project?

Data & Visualization

- Is the data already available? If not, when will it be ready?
- Where does the data come from?
- Do you expect any incompleteness or known limitations?
- About how much data is there?
- What format is it in?
- Will the data be changing and will you need access to edit it yourself?
- Do you already have a preferred encoding method/ chart type in mind?
- Is there a chart type that you absolutely don't want to use?
- What would you want a reader to take away if they only had 5 seconds?

Design Specifications

- Is this part of a larger project?
- Do you have brand guidelines to follow?
- What is the medium for the project? Static, interactive, web, print …
- Any specific formats or sizes?
- Are you considering using the graphics in multiple mediums? (like social media, animated video)
- Are there any accessibility concerns?
- Are there any colors that you absolutely hate?

- Are there any visual elements that you want to include specifically? (e.g., people, icons, photography, patterns?)

Art Direction

- In a few words …
  - What are your organization's core values?
  - How would your audience or community describe you?
  - How would you describe your audience?
  - How do people feel after interacting with you?
  - What value do you deliver to others?
  - How are you different than your competition?
- What emotion do you want your audience to feel when they view the project?

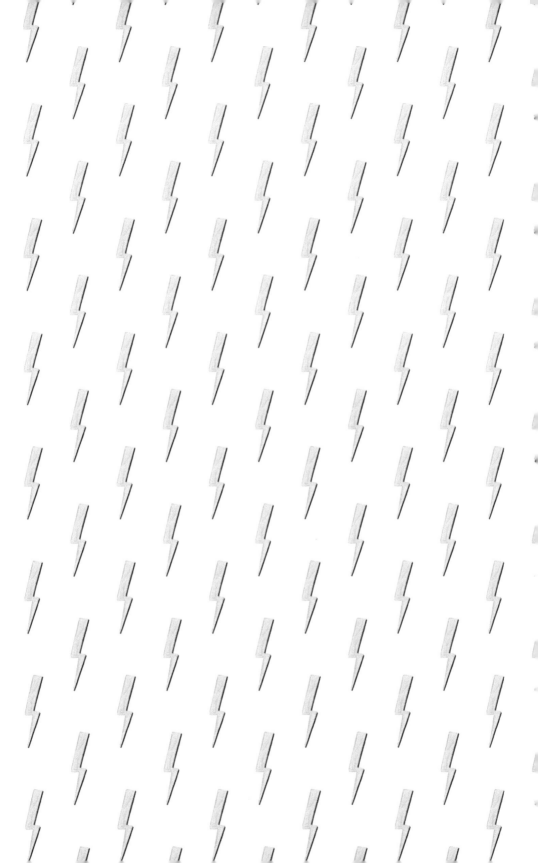

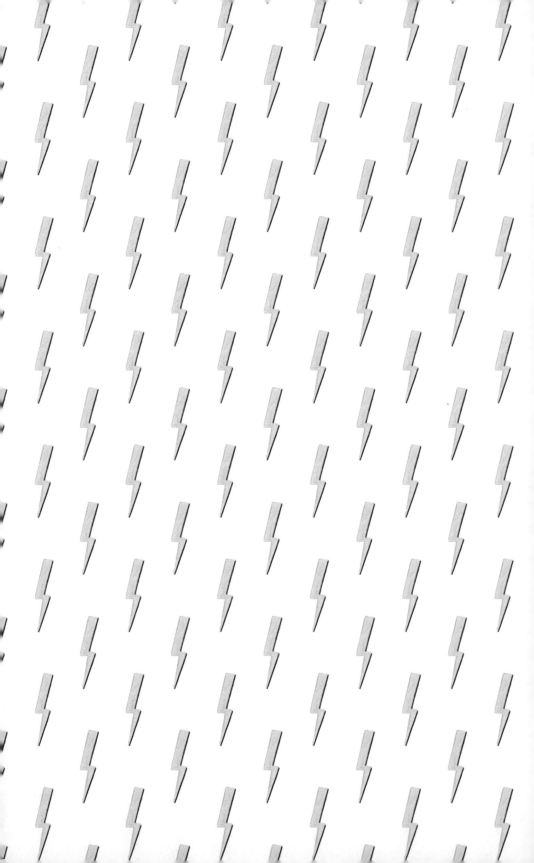

Made in the USA
Columbia, SC
16 December 2023

28701324R00089